PAUL HARRISON

ULTIMATE
FOOTBALL HEROES

WREXHAM AFC

FROM THE PLAYGROUND
TO THE PITCH

DINO

First published by Dino Books in 2023,
an imprint of Bonnier Books UK,
4th Floor, Victoria House, Bloomsbury Square, London WC1B 4DA
Owned by Bonnier Books,
Sveavägen 56, Stockholm, Sweden

© X @UFHbooks
www.heroesfootball.com
www.bonnierbooks.co.uk

Text © Studio Press 2023

Paperback ISBN: 978 1 78946 766 6
E-book ISBN: 978 1 78946 793 2

British Library cataloguing-in-publication data:
A catalogue record for this book is available from the British Library.

Printed and bound in Great Britain by Clays Ltd, Elcograf S.p.A.

1 3 5 7 9 10 8 6 4 2

For Sue.

The game would not have been
the same without you.

Paul Harrison was born in Newcastle-upon-Tyne and grew up in County Durham. This left him with an accent that people find trustworthy, so surveys have confirmed. It also left him with an allegiance to Newcastle United football club. Newcastle won their last major trophy months before he was born. In bleak moments, he wonders if this is his fault.

After a degree in Southampton he worked in a variety of different jobs with mixed success. He's been a labourer for a roofer (he was rubbish at that), a labourer for a builder (he was keen, but also rubbish), a waiter (really rubbish) and a barman (merely adequate). He's sold double glazing (uselessly), toys (not badly), and garden furniture (all right at that). Since then, he's been a children's books editor (passable at that, actually) and now he teaches as well as writing books for what may loosely be described as a living.

Paul lives with his wife and two children in West Sussex.

Cover illustration by Dan Leydon.
To learn more about Dan, visit danleydon.com
To purchase his artwork visit etsy.com/shop/footynews
Or just follow him on Twitter @danleydon

TABLE OF CONTENTS

ACKNOWLEDGEMENTS

I would like to thank Emil, the editor of this book and
a man I once shared an office with many years ago.
He remains one of the most drily amusing and capable
people I have had the pleasure to work with.

CHAPTER 1

PENALTY HERO

10 April 2023, Racecourse Ground

The referee blew his whistle and pointed to the penalty spot. A confused silence settled over the Wrexham fans, but the away supporters from Notts County were overjoyed. This was a must-win game and their side had been given a lifeline. Wrexham were 3–2 up in the final seconds of the match before a desperate corner had led to the ball hitting Eoghan O'Connell's arm – and the referee had given County a penalty for handball!

"He can't give that!" fumed the Wrexham manager, Phil Parkinson. "It was from point-blank range – what was he meant to do with his arm?"

On the pitch, the players couldn't believe it either.

"Don't worry, mate," said Luke Young, the Wrexham captain, to Eoghan. "That's a harsh decision, there's nothing you could have done there."

Eoghan nodded, but inside he felt gutted because he knew how important this game was. There was only one automatic promotion spot available from this league, and Notts County were Wrexham's closest rivals. Both teams were tied at the top of the table on an amazing 100 points – well clear of the chasing pack – but a draw away from home would be a better result for County than for Wrexham. Eoghan trudged, miserably, to the 18-yard line of the box to await the spot kick.

Although most of the Wrexham players were either disappointed or annoyed, there was one who was calm – and maybe even a little excited. The Wrexham keeper, Ben Foster, had seen and done everything there was to do across his long career in football. He had played over 500 games for teams such as Manchester United, West Bromwich Albion and

Watford; he had even kept goal for England!

Ben knew that when it came to penalties the pressure was on the player taking the kick, not the goalkeeper, because everyone expects the penalty-taker to score. He knew what all goalkeepers knew – this was his chance to be a hero.

"You alright Ben?" Luke asked, slapping his keeper on the back.

"'Course I am," smiled Ben. "Don't worry lads, I've got this covered."

Luke chuckled to himself and jogged back to his place on the line. It was a good feeling knowing you had Ben Foster in goal. It was also reassuring to know that Ben took his training seriously, and that included researching what players did when they took penalties.

Ben had been preparing for just this situation. Before each game he and the coaches had gone through what kind of kick each team's penalty-taker would try; usually, players took the same kind of kick every time and only practised that.

Even though County's usual penalty-taker, Ruben Rodrigues, had been subbed off earlier in the game,

Ben was confident he knew where any other player they chose would put it. He calmly took a sip from his water bottle as he watched Cedwyn Scott walk up and place the ball on the penalty spot.

The Racecourse Ground fell into a deathly silence. It felt like everyone was holding their breath.

He's going to place it to my left, thought Ben, recalling what Aidan Davison, the goalkeeping coach, had said to him pre-game.

But then Ben looked again. Cedwyn wasn't looking so confident. Ben stood to his full 1.93m height and stretched his arms out wide to try and fill as much as the goal as possible and intimidate the Notts County player. He had a good feeling in the pit of his stomach.

Cedwyn took a few paces back, glanced up at the goal and slowly exhaled to calm his nerves. The referee, Scott Tallis, put the whistle to his lips and blew. Cedwyn paused and then started his run-up – but something didn't look right.

Ben saw it immediately: *he's changed his penalty; he's going to put it to my right!* Quick as a flash, Ben adjusted his feet and pushed off in the opposite direction to the one he was originally going to take.

Cedwyn hit the ball well, strong and hard; but Ben had chosen correctly. The ball thudded into Ben's left wrist, cannoned away, and was kicked to safety for a corner.

Yeeeeessssssssssss!!!! The ground erupted with the roar of the crowd.

The Wrexham team mobbed their penalty hero. Ben had a grin from ear to ear as he picked himself up.

"Right, focus lads!" shouted Luke. "We've still got this corner to deal with!"

The referee glanced at his watch. There were seconds left. This was County's last chance to salvage a point – Wrexham had to stand firm! The corner was swung in, headed in the air, headed again, and finally hooked away upfield. The referee put the whistle to his lips and blew – the game was over! The crowd roared their approval again.

Wrexham were three points clear at the top of the table – the league was almost in their grasp!

CHAPTER 2

TWO SEASONS EARLIER

7 March 2020, Racecourse Ground

The 2019–20 season had promised so much for Wrexham AFC – but it was delivering the exact opposite. The manager, Dean Keates, had reason to believe that this would be the year that they would finally win promotion from the National League. Wrexham had spent 10 years there already – one of the longest stays of any team in the division – and it was not where a team with Wrexham's history, the proud Red Dragons of North Wales, should be playing.

The problem was, there was only one automatic promotion spot into the football league, and another one via the play-offs. Many people thought that it was the hardest league to get promoted from. The season before, Wrexham had come close, but had lost out in the play-offs.

This season had to be better, didn't it?

The short answer was no. A poor start had seen the previous manager sacked after just seven weeks. Dean had been brought in to improve matters, but things had gone from bad to worse.

By the end of November, Wrexham were bottom of the league. Things picked up slightly, but Wrexham still hadn't managed to string together more than two wins in a row. By the beginning of March, the team were only a couple of points above the relegation places. They badly needed a win, and the game against Eastleigh seemed as good a chance as any.

"Come on boys," said Dean as he addressed the team in the changing room before the match. "Eastleigh are only one place above us – win this and we can start putting some distance between us and the teams below us. Let's do what we do well and get the result we need."

Wrexham's current position was as much a puzzle to the team captain, Shaun Pearson, as anyone. At the start of the season, he'd been confident that Wrexham would make the play-offs at the very least. The results had been a worry, but the team spirit wasn't bad – he knew they'd give each game a good go.

"Let's get into them boys," he shouted. "They're there for the taking!" Shaun clapped his hands loudly as the team got to their feet, their studs clattering over the changing room floor as they headed for the pitch.

Eastleigh – or the Spitfires, as they were known – might have been at the wrong end of the table, like Wrexham were, but they were no pushovers. The Spitfires were a skilful side that should have been pushing for promotion.

The game was a scrappy affair. Wrexham thought they'd gone ahead in the second half when striker Jordan Ponticelli headed in from a cross, but the goal was ruled out for offside. The game finished in a disappointing 0–0 draw, with as many yellow cards as shots on target.

A chorus of boos rang around the Racecourse

Ground when the final whistle blew. The crowd might have been small that day, but they made their feelings known on how the season was going.

What the supporters didn't realise at the time was that this was going to be the last game that Wrexham were going to play that season. Football was going to lose out to the global Covid-19 pandemic.

The League took a vote and decided to stop the season early. It was a mess. Teams had played different numbers of games, so it was difficult to find a fair way of working out who was to be promoted and who would be relegated.

In the end it was decided that teams would get an average points-per-game score. Wrexham finished with an average score of 1.16 points per game, which left them in 20th place – three places above the relegation places. In a season that had promised promotion, in the end they were lucky not to be relegated.

But Covid-19 was not the only thing that would surprise the long-suffering Wrexham supporters. Strange as it might have seemed, across the Atlantic Ocean there were people planning to buy a football club in Britain, and had decided Wrexham was the team they would go for.

Their identity was going to surprise not just the Wrexham fans, but the footballing world in general. A bit of Hollywood glamour was about to be sprinkled over the crumbling stands of the Racecourse Ground.

CHAPTER 3

AN ENGLISHMAN ABROAD

Humphrey Ker was enjoying life. A British actor, writer
and comedian, Humphrey was appearing in a TV
show called *Mythic Quest* created by his friend, the
TV star Rob McElhenney, who was best known for
his hit show *It's Always Sunny in Philadelphia*. Part of
their friendship was based on the fact Humphrey and
Rob were both massive sports fans. Rob followed his
hometown American football team, the Philadelphia
Eagles, while Humphrey was a huge Liverpool
fan. Rob would often see his friend catching up on
Liverpool games during their breaks. Rob didn't follow
"soccer", as he called it, and wasn't really sure what
was going on, so Humphrey would explain what was

happening, pointing out all the little details that made it such an exciting game.

"You should watch *Sunderland 'til I Die*," Humphrey told Rob. "It's a decent documentary series about supporting a struggling football team."

Rob was interested. He loved finding out about new things and the fact that this was about sport made it even better. Little did either of them know, but he would have the perfect opportunity to watch it – filming on *Mythic Quest* was to be shut down because of the Covid-19 outbreak. Rob would have all the time in the world.

When Rob and Humphrey finally got back together, Rob was raving about the documentary. He'd watched the whole series in two days – one minute he was in tears, the next he was jumping off his seat and cheering!

"I never realised soccer could grab people like that!" he told Humphrey.

"Well, I'm glad you liked it – now you see why I'm so keen on watching football," Humphrey replied. "I've often thought it would be great to own a football club."

"Funny you should say that," Rob replied, "but I've decided I want one."

"Want a what?" asked Humphrey. "You don't mean a football club?"

Rob did. He understood, now, what football meant to people. And he wanted to be involved with a club that was really important to their community – somewhere that he could make better, both for the club and the people who live there.

"Are you serious?" asked Humphrey, but he knew the answer already. His friend had that look in his eye that he knew meant business. Rob was incredibly hard-working and driven. If he wanted something badly enough, he would move Heaven and Earth to get it.

"Yeah, I'm deadly serious," Rob replied.

"I'm not being funny or anything, Rob," said Humphrey, "but you don't know anything about running a football club. Or buying one for that matter."

"No, of course not. I know that," laughed Rob. "That's why you're going to help me!"

"I'm going to what?" exclaimed Humphrey. "Look Rob, I like my football, but that doesn't mean I know anything about any of that stuff either!"

"Yeah, but you're a clever man – you'll know where to look," Rob replied, slapping his friend on the back. "Find me a good one."

Easier said than done, thought Humphrey. *Where do I even start?*

CHAPTER 4

THE OLDEST CLUB IN WALES

Rob wanted to buy a club that wasn't doing so well, so he could improve them. This was good news – a struggling club was likely to be cheaper than a successful one. The question was, which club? Humphrey scratched his head – how do you decide which club to buy? And how much does buying a football club even cost? Clearly the thought of purchasing a Premier League club was a non-starter for all sorts of reasons, not least the price tag. No, Humphrey knew he would be looking at the lower reaches of the Football League pyramid. He quickly realised he needed to make a checklist of what Rob wanted in a club and what each club could offer.

Humphrey made a list of important things he would have to consider when looking for which team to buy:

- History – the club had to be well established, with its own sense of identity and a with a story behind it. What challenges had the club faced? Who were its heroes?
- Fanbase – there had to be a good number of loyal, dedicated fans and the promise that this number might easily increase very quickly when the club became more successful.
- Facilities – did the club own its own ground? Were there decent training facilities? Would the ground need lots of money spent on it?
- Finance – the club shouldn't be loaded with debt, or really struggling to pay its bills. Would it be attractive to sponsors when it became more successful? Were there any easy ways of increasing the income the club could make? Also, importantly, how much would the club cost?
- Geography – was the club surrounded by much bigger and more successful sides?

Writing that list was the easy bit – now Humphrey

had to find clubs that would match what he was after. He spent hours looking at league tables, maps and statistics – he even used the computer game *Football Manager* to find out more. But it was clear he needed some proper, professional help. Humphrey got in touch with a company called Inner Circle Sports. They had helped arrange the buying and selling of Liverpool football club, as well as Portsmouth – just the kind of experts Humphrey needed.

During the search some famous names cropped up, such as Bolton Wanderers and Wigan Athletic. It was tempting to be involved with clubs like that, but they were just too big. Their facilities were too good – what could Rob do with clubs like that to improve them? No, Humphrey needed something smaller, but just as exciting. One club was standing out from all the others – Wrexham!

Wrexham Association Football Club – to give it its full name – or the Red Dragons, as they were nicknamed, was ticking all the right boxes on Humphrey's list. Wrexham played their first football game in 1864, which made them not only the oldest football club in Wales, but the third oldest club in the world. They had never played in the top division of the league, but this didn't mean they hadn't had a successful and inspiring history. They had won the Welsh Cup a record 23 times, along with winning the Football League Trophy and the FA Trophy. Wrexham had won the third division (now League One) and had qualified for Europe on more than one occasion – even beating some of the great sides, such as Porto of Portugal. In their best European run Wrexham got to the quarter-finals of the Cup Winner's Cup in the 1975/76 season.

There were great stories and great players. The clip of Mickey Thomas's winning free kick against Arsenal in the FA Cup in 1992 was still shown regularly on TV, and older Wrexham fans would remember favourite players such as Alan Kennedy, Brian Horne and Joey Jones. Humphrey knew Rob would like this part of the club's folklore.

That wasn't the end of the history either – Wrexham's home, the Racecourse Ground, was the oldest international stadium still in use in the entire world! True, it was looking worse for wear these days, and one of the stands was too unsafe to use – but this meant that there were things that Rob could improve.

Wrexham's geographical position was also in its favour. There were no other big clubs right next door. True, Liverpool and Everton weren't too far away, but far enough for there to be strong local support for the team. Although Wrexham's crowds weren't huge, they were big for a club stuck in the National League – and there was plenty to suggest the crowds would grow with the promise of success.

Wrexham were the team – but were they for sale?

CHAPTER 5

ENTER DEADPOOL

"Humphrey, I love it!" said Rob. "Wrexham is the perfect club! How much?"

Humphrey thought it would cost around £2 million, or $2.4 million. That would cover the cost, with a little bit left over for improving the team, or any emergency spending. "But that's if you can convince them to sell," he said. "It's owned by a supporter's group. They control it now, after a previous owner sold off the ground and nearly got the club closed down. As a result, they're a bit wary of what a new owner might end up doing."

"Yeah, that makes sense," said Rob. "$2.4 million is a lot of cash. Too much for me – but I know someone who might help out."

"Who's that?" asked Humphrey.

"Ryan Reynolds," said Rob with a smile.

"What? The guy who played Deadpool?"
asked Humphrey.

"The one and the same. We need Hollywood money
for a deal like this. Leave it with me."

Rob had known Ryan for a number of years. They'd
never worked together; Rob worked in TV, whereas
Ryan worked in movies. In fact they'd never even
met each other in real life, but they had called and
messaged each other many times in the past. Ryan also
had a good eye for business and had invested in lots
of different projects over the years; would investing in
Wrexham be of interest to the Canadian film star?

Although Ryan had played lots of sports of a child,
including ice hockey, he wasn't much of a sports fan.
Rob knew that to get Ryan involved he would have to
sell the idea to Ryan as a project with a story, not just
as a business idea. Rob told Ryan about the club and
the area and, importantly, about how a team could be
promoted or relegated. Although there was nothing

unusual about this for football fans across the world, in North American sports such as American football, baseball and basketball, promotion and relegation are virtually unheard of. The idea that a team could move up to the top league – or go in the opposite direction – really interested Ryan.

What Ryan even more interesting though was the idea that his money could make a real difference to a town, not just a team. Having a successful club would help Wrexham in lots of different ways, and that appealed to him most of all.

"So – are you on board?" asked Rob.

"Yes, I'm in. My word, what have I just agreed to," chuckled Ryan. "I should have known not to take your call; you just won't stop until you get what you want."

"You know me too well!" laughed Rob. "Right then, let's get this done."

Getting it done wasn't going to be as straightforward as buying any other club. Wrexham wasn't owned by one person or company; it was owned by a group of supporters, the Wrexham Supporters Trust. These fans had saved their club by raising enough money to take it over, in 2011, when it was in severe financial difficulty – and they weren't about to let just anybody buy it, particularly if they seemed to be buying it as a hobby.

The Supporters Trust would vote on any deal being made for the club. If the idea didn't get 75% of the votes, then the deal was dead. Rob and Ryan would be back to square one, and Humphrey would be looking for a new club.

"What happens if we don't get enough votes?" Ryan worried.

"Well, we could try buying Hartlepool. They came pretty close to Wrexham when I was looking before," Humphrey replied.

"No, we all know this is the one," said Rob. "We've just got to convince the group that we have the best interests of Wrexham at heart. We know that it's about the community as well as the club. We've got to prove to them that we get that. I understand these people – they're like the people I grew up with in Philadelphia. I know what their club means to them. I know how winning affects a community."

"Then all we need to do is convince the Supporters Trust that we're genuine," said Humphrey.

"Yes, tell them we're not going to take this responsibility lightly," said Ryan. He paused a moment. "I don't think I've ever been this nervous," he said. "I'm actually sweating!"

Rob laughed. "We can do this. Let's go."

Rob and Ryan logged into the Zoom meeting and in a long conversation between North Wales and the East and West coasts of America, dreams and plans were discussed between two American stars and a group of dedicated Wrexham supporters. Then, the votes were cast.

CHAPTER 6

A NEW DAWN

As expected, most of the Trust had logged into the meeting to hear the pitch from the American stars. What wasn't quite as expected was how well Rob and Ryan had done in convincing them that they genuinely had Wrexham's best interests at heart. Over 98% of the votes cast were in favour of Rob and Ryan taking over. The Trust members were impressed by Rob and Ryan's vision of the future. Their plans were sensible and realistic, even if Ryan did dream of the club one day being in the Premier League!

Their first job was to get promoted out of the National League and into Division 2 – the lowest division of the proper Football League. When the news got out that the club had been bought, fans gathered outside the ground, lit fireworks and danced and sang. One person was even dressed as Ryan's superhero movie character Deadpool. For them it felt like the good times were coming back to Wrexham. There was one problem though...

"Well, the vote went well, but the truth is we don't have a clue about how to run a professional football club," said Humphrey.

"Humphrey, we're going to need you to go there and act as our eyes and ears," said Rob. "Also, to let everyone at the club know that we're not going to start changing things for the sake of it. They're probably worried about what's going to happen."

It was true. Buying a club was completely different to running a club. They weren't the only ones having doubts about their chances of making a success of things. The Wrexham football team weren't convinced either. The changing room was buzzing with speculation and questions.

"So who's bought it?"

"It's Russell Crowe, I think."

"What the *Gladiator* guy?"

"Nah, it's Ryan Reynolds."

"And that one from that TV programme. You know the one about sunny Philadelphia."

"Philadelphia cheese?"

"No, the American sitcom. I quite like it."

"Never heard of it."

"Are you sure it's not Russell Crowe?"

"Doesn't matter who it is – I want to know what's going to happen."

"You're just worried they're going to sign Mbappé or Messi."

Everyone laughed.

"Imagine Ronaldo at the chippy!"

"Okay boys, settle down," said Dean Keates, the manager. "We'll find out soon enough what the new owners are going to be like, but we've got a game this weekend, so we need to get focused on that. As far as I'm concerned, everything else is just a distraction."

Dean was right: there *had* been a lot of distractions. There had been rumours of a takeover for a while. A huge white sign made up of letters spelling

"WREXHAM" had appeared on a local hill, just like the famous Hollywood sign in Los Angeles. It was only natural that people would be excited at a bit of movie magic happening in North Wales.

There was also the small matter of a film crew popping up around the ground. They were filming the takeover for a documentary series. Rob and Ryan had agreed to it as the money it brought in would help pay for the club and give their team some global publicity. It was a win-win situation for them, but it made life a little awkward if you were trying, like Dean, to get a team of footballers to concentrate on an upcoming game.

When Humphrey arrived, he could sense that everyone at the club – not least the players – would need reassuring that Wrexham was in good hands. The good news was Humphrey had someone in mind: Shaun Harvey. Shaun had decades of experience in football; he had worked at both Bradford and Leeds United football clubs, as well as spending years in a senior role at the Football League. He agreed to join Wrexham as an advisor, to help them get the show on the road, and to use his contacts and knowledge to make sure they were hiring the right people at the right price.

The next important person to be hired was the Chief Executive – the person in charge of the day to day running of the club. One person fitted the bill perfectly: Fleur Robinson. She had been on the board at Burton Albion football club, so she understood the world that Wrexham found themselves in. She wasn't going to be blinded by the Hollywood glamour, and she would do the important jobs that would give Wrexham the best chance of fulfilling Rob and Ryan's dreams.

The pieces of the jigsaw were falling into place – now it was up to the team to do their bit and win promotion.

CHAPTER 7

DISAPPOINTMENT

29 May 2021, Victoria Ground

In the end, they just couldn't do it. The new era at the Racecourse Ground started brightly with a 2–0 win over Woking. But the very next game it all came crashing down with a 3–0 away defeat to Aldershot. And a goalless home draw with Hartlepool wasn't giving them the push up the table that they needed.

This became the pattern for the rest of the season – a couple of rousing wins before a defeat and a draw that would slow their push for promotion. Despite this stop-start run, the Red Dragons were still moving in the right direction; they were in the play-off positions as the season drew to a close. Their final home game was a cracking 5–3 win against King's Lynn. This meant that if they won the last game of the season away to Dagenham and Redbridge they'd be guaranteed a place in the play-offs!

Dagenham and Redbridge were mid-table and had no hope of reaching the play-offs; basically, their season was over. The Wrexham supporters were hoping that their opponents might have switched off a bit and wouldn't be trying particularly hard. However, the opposite seemed to be true. Dagenham and Redbridge were playing with the freedom that comes when you've got nothing to lose. The first half passed, and Wrexham hadn't managed to put their stamp on the game. It was like they were letting the pressure get to them.

"We're letting the pressure get to us," fumed Dean Keates at half time. "Play the game, not the occasion. You've got to get the basics right! Do the simple things well and we can win this!"

Unfortunately, when the second half started there was no improvement in Wrexham's game. They were still sloppy in possession and were making poor choices on the ball. Then in the 51st minute disaster happened – Dagenham and Redbridge went 1–0 up. The promotion place was slipping through Wrexham's fingers!

What could be worse than this? Wrexham were about to find out. Just five minutes later Wrexham's Paul Rutherford was shown a straight red card for a dangerous tackle. Wrexham were down to ten men! §

"We've got to go for it now," Dean shouted. "Push up, push up!"

Wrexham gave it everything, but nothing worked. The ball wouldn't stick at the right time and chances went begging. The clock was ticking down and the supporters began to fear the worst.

"Come on Wrexham!" they shouted.

And then, in the 90th minute, a lifeline! Jordan Ponticelli slotted home!

GOOOOOOOAAAAAAAAAALLLLLLLLLL!

Wrexham were back in the game!

"Let's make this count!" screamed Dean, clapping his hands loudly.

The referee blew the whistle to restart the match. Even though they were down to ten men, Wrexham were full of belief; however, they knew that time was against them. Wrexham poured forward, but the ball would not drop for them. Things were getting desperate – they needed that second goal! The fans wanted time to slow down, but time waits for no one. With grim inevitability the referee put the whistle to his lips and blew. The game was over – the players dropped to their knees. They had failed!

There was one slim chance – Wrexham might still get into the play-off positions if other results went their way.

"What's the Chesterfield score?" asked Dean. If Chesterfield won, they would go above Wrexham in the league.

"They won," replied assistant Andy Davies grimly. "Bromley are winning too."

Dean understood what this meant. Wrexham would finish the season in eighth place: one place below the play-offs. Their season was over. Wrexham were still stuck in the National League. Like the long-suffering

Wrexham supporters, Rob and Ryan's dreams had turned to dust. Real life had intruded into the fairy-tale and it didn't feel good.

Wrexham had to take stock and do it all over again.

CHAPTER 8

WE'VE GOT MULLIN

Staying in the National League for another season wasn't just a disappointment. There were bigger, more serious consequences. The club was losing money every year that it played at this level. Eventually, drastic action might have to be taken – people could lose their jobs and livelihoods. This in turn could have a knock-on effect: every bit of cost cutting meant it would be a little harder to get promotion. Something had to change.

Unfortunately for Dean Keates and his staff, they were the first change. The board felt that their best bet for getting promoted next season would be to have a new manager with different ideas in charge, so Dean

and his two assistants left the club. They were not the
only people to say goodbye to the Racecourse Ground;
a clutch of players, including the unfortunate Paul
Rutherford, who had been sent off in his last game,
were also released.

Obviously, with so many people leaving,
replacements would have to be found – the manager
in particular. It was the key role, and one the board
had to get right. Of course, with Wrexham's celebrity
owners giving the club having a much higher profile
than other National League sides, there was a lot of
interest in the role. Over 100 applications arrived at
the Racecourse Ground, but the board was interested
in one name in particular. The only problem was, he
hadn't applied!

Phil Parkinson was a well-known figure in the
Football League. He had won three promotions in
his career and was the only manager to have taken
a League 2 side to the final of the League Cup. In
the past Phil had managed teams such as Bolton
and Bradford, and had taken Colchester to the
Championship. Phil was out of work at the time,

taking a break since leaving the managerial merry-go-round that was Sunderland. However, he was experienced and ambitious, and Shaun wasn't sure that Wrexham would be of interest.

"I don't know, Humphrey. I think he'd be looking at teams in higher leagues than us," said Shaun.

"Sure, I get that," Humphrey replied, "but it's worth a phone call, isn't it?"

"Definitely," said Fleur. "You don't get anything if you don't ask."

"Then we're agreed, Let's give it a go."

Phil said no. First of all, he was being asked to drop out of the Football League and go down to the National League. Secondly, he was suspicious of a club with celebrity owners. *Will they get bored of it?* he wondered. *Is this just some kind of hobby? In 18 months are they just going to up sticks and leave?*

He was also aware of how much rebuilding had to be done. Nearly half the playing staff had been released or had left and Phil knew what the financial realities were in the National League. Money would be tight – even with rich owners.

Humphrey explained Phil's decision to Rob when they met up next in Los Angeles.

"Do you think I could speak to him?" asked Rob. "Could you fix up a phone call?"

Humphrey knew how persuasive Rob could be. If anyone could get Phil to change his mind it would be Rob.

"I could try..." Humphrey replied.

The call was made. It was like the meeting with the Supporters Trust all over again. Rob had to prove that he and Ryan were in this for the long haul, and it wasn't some kind of gimmick, or a new toy they would get tired of. The call worked – Phil agreed to join the club and be part of the Wrexham rebuild.

His first job was to work on the playing staff. When preseason training started it was his first real chance to see how good his squad was, and do his best to improve them as players. Phil knew this would be the cheapest way to make his team better – at this level, saving money for top quality signings would be the name of the game.

Wrexham did need to make signings, too, though, otherwise the squad would have been too thin. The name that was exciting the fans' social media groups was Paul Mullin.

Paul was the star striker for Cambridge United, who had just been promoted that season to League 1. Paul had finished the season as the league's top scorer with 32 goals, and had scored 34 goals in all competitions – he was a goal-scoring machine. There was also a rumour that Paul would like to move to a club closer to his home city of Liverpool. The question was, would a striker of Paul's quality be likely to drop down two leagues to play for Wrexham? The fans weren't so sure.

"Why on earth would Mullin come here? He should be playing for a Championship side," said one.

"Don't underestimate the pull of family," said another. "He's got young kids – maybe he wants to be near their grandparents."

Remarkably, the club managed to persuade Paul to join. There was further good news: Paul was out of contract at Cambridge, so there was no transfer fee to pay. He was going to be the highest paid player in the squad, but goal-scorers always cost more than any other player. Goals win games and no one scored goals like 'Super' Paul Mullin.

They had a top manager and a top goalscorer now. Things were changing all over the club. There were new sponsors, and even the away strip had been changed to match the colours of the Philadelphia Eagles American Football team, in honour of Rob's hometown side. The sales of the replica strips were over ten times higher than the previous year.

Wrexham were ready for the new season!

CHAPTER 9

HIGHS AND LOWS

30 August 2021, Racecourse Ground

A real sense of excitement was building around the club when the new season kicked off. Season ticket sales were through the roof and the fans were about to come flooding back to the Racecourse Ground. The ground had been closed to spectators during the Covid-19 pandemic; now the fans were desperate to be back in the stadium. This was good news for the club – more fans meant more money was coming in for all the improvements they had to make. The players preferred playing in front of their own fans, too – the noisy Wrexham supporters were vital to giving the players a lift and putting their opponents off.

One of the most expensive changes that took place over the off-season was laying a new pitch. The Red Dragons were a skilful footballing side, so having a decent pitch was going to be an advantage. The stadium had been given a lick of paint, too, so the old ground was looking better than it had for years. The only problem was that Wrexham's first two games were away from home, so the fans had another week and a half to wait before cheering on their team.

This was bad news for the team, too. Playing away from home is harder than playing in front of your own fans; and so it proved for Wrexham. The first game of the season was a frustrating 2–2 draw at Solihull Moors. New signing Paul had got off the mark with his first goal for Wrexham, but they had conceded an injury time equaliser, turning three valuable points into one. It got better in the next game, with a 2–0 win at old rivals Eastleigh – Jake Hyde bagging two goals as the Wrexham defence kept a clean sheet against the Spitfires.

Finally, it was time for the first home game of the

season, and it was against one of the strongest sides in the division – Notts County. Like Wrexham, most fans thought they were too big a club to be down in the National League. County, nicknamed the Magpies after their black and white strip, were the oldest professional club in the entire world, and were one of the original founding teams of the very first football league. Although they had never won the top division title, in the past they had won every other league championship, to go along with winning the FA Cup.

It was true that over the years their success had been a bit hit and miss, but most people felt there was something sad about seeing this famous old club stuck in the National League. However, County's manager, Ian Burchnall, had put together a strong team and they would be battling hard for that automatic promotion spot.

The game kicked off in front of a raucous home crowd and Wrexham were quickly into their promotion rivals. Paul latched onto a wayward defensive header and surged between the retreating Magpie defenders.

"Come on Paul!" roared the crowd.

Without breaking stride Paul lashed a left foot shot goalward from the left side of the box, but the County keeper saved.

"He's looking sharp again," said Phil, smiling to his assistant Steve Parkin.

The match went back and forth, with both sides having chances. Luke hit one over from a good position, but County were still threatening on the break. Then, in the 25th minute, Wrexham crossed the ball into the box from the right-hand side. Jake jumped with his back to goal and sent a clever, cushioned header back into the centre of the box where James Jones smashed the ball home.

GOOOOOAAAAAAAALLLLLLLL!!!!!

"Yes! Beautiful strike Jonesy!" shouted Paul, congratulating his fellow forward.

But joy turned to despair – the assistant referee had their flag raised for off-side!

"Oh, that's got be tight!" fumed Phil on the sidelines.

It was about to get worse. On the stroke of half time

County forward Kyle Wootton got on the end of a long cross and headed past Wrexham keeper, Rob Lainton, to score his third goal in three games. Wrexham were 1–0 down with it all to do in the second half. This was not the homecoming the fans had hoped for.

The second half started like the first. Wrexham piled on the early pressure and just a couple of minutes after the restart the ball was crossed into the County box. Paul powered between the defenders and buried his header in the back of the net.

GOOOOOAAAAAAAALLLLLLLL!!!!!

This time there was no flag to spoil the celebrations!

The home fans were seeing first-hand that Paul's reputation was completely justified.

"What a player that Mullin is!" one shouted over the noise.

We've got Mullin, super Paul Mullin… the chant rang round the Racecourse Ground.

"Let's hope we hear a lot more of that," joked Phil to the rest of the home dugout.

There would be no more goals that day unfortunately. A late chance for Wrexham to nab all three points came in the final seconds, but Max Cleworth's flicked header was deflected away. The whistle went to end the game. Five points from the first three games; not a bad return, but a clear indication that this season was going to be tough – even with super Paul Mullin in the team.

CHAPTER 10

A DAY TO REMEMBER

30 October 2021, Racecourse Ground

The game against Torquay United was the closest home game to Remembrance Sunday, so the club solemnly paid their respects to those that had died during armed conflicts around the world. The two club captains placed poppy wreaths on the centre circle before the game, and a minute's silence was held to remember the dead. It was a day to remember for other reasons, too – it was the first home game the club's new owners had been to since the take-over.

There was a record crowd to welcome Rob and Ryan, who had both flown over earlier that week.

They had been at Wrexham's battling 3–2 loss away at Maidenhead, where they saw Wrexham come back from 2–0 down to level the game despite being down to ten men. Unfortunately, Maidenhead had gone on to win, but now was a chance to put things right at home. The Racecourse Ground was rocking as the fans chanted Rob and Ryan's names before the game. Their look of pride and joy was as bright as the floodlights. If they had ever doubted their decision to buy the club, then it was made clear they had made the right choice now.

It wasn't quite the perfect occasion; Paul was suspended, bringing an end to his run of scoring in the last five games. Wrexham didn't seem to be missing their nine-goal leading striker though, when they went ahead in the fourth minute! Captain Ben Tozer took one of his trademark long throws from the left touchline. The ball looped into the Torquay box and bounced kindly for the unmarked Wrexham defender Harry Lennon to slash the ball home.

GOOOOOAAAAAAAALLLLLLLL!!!!!

The crowd – including the A-list owners – went

berserk. What a start!

"Beautiful goal!" shouted Ben.

"You keep setting them up like that and I'll keep knocking them in," laughed Harry. "Honestly Ben, this goal scoring carry on is dead easy – I don't know why Mullin gets all the glory!"

Ben laughed as he lined up for the game to kick off again.

Wrexham kept on pressing but couldn't get that vital second goal. Chances came and went – flicked attempts went wide, or the ball wouldn't drop quite right for the strikers. The game continued like that into the second half until Bryce Hosannah drove into the box and was brought down by the Torquay defender!

"Penalty!" screamed Phil from the touchline. Behind him in the directors' seats the owners held their breath, unsure what would happen, swept along by the explosion of noise from the crowd. Unbelievably, the referee waved play on!

"Ref!" Phil shouted. "That was a nailed-on penalty!"

The referee didn't like the Wrexham manager's

tone and Phil's name went into the book. There was no time to hang about arguing about the decision, though. There was no Video Assistant Referee in the National League and Torquay were on the attack. Wrexham cleared the ball, but another chance had slipped away. Would these missed opportunities come back to haunt the Red Dragons?

The fans were right to worry. Against the run of play Torquay scored an equalizer in the 84th minute. Conceding a goal so late in the game left Wrexham little time to get the win they wanted. Dior Angus flashed a shot wide in the dying moments, but that was as close as they came. After leading the game for so long a draw felt really disappointing – especially with the owners watching. It would have been good to send them back to the United States having seen their team win.

It was still a valuable point though; and who knew how important that might be at the end of the season?

CHAPTER 11

EXCITING TIMES

Rob and Ryan should have hung around a little bit longer. Wrexham went on a great run of form for the remaining nine games of 2021, only dropping five points and securing 22, with seven wins and a draw. In amongst those wins were a thumping 5–0 victory away at Aldershot and a 6–2 drubbing of King's Lynn at their own ground. The defence was doing their bit for the team too, with Wrexham only conceding five goals in that period.

"If you don't concede, you don't lose," as Phil would tell his team.

These were exciting times both on and off the field. There were more new sponsors announced –

which was handy as the pitch had to be re-laid again, at great expense, when the new pitch started to fall apart. Although laying the new pitch was a big hole in the club's budget – it cost £100,000 to get it done – this figure would be dwarfed by Wrexham's biggest purchase. The club were going to try and buy the stadium.

When Humphrey Ker was making his list of potential clubs to buy, there were two areas where Wrexham scored poorly – they didn't own a training ground and, more importantly, they didn't own the Racecourse Ground. This meant that the club couldn't replace the closed Kop stand, which was too unsafe to use and had stood empty and derelict for years. The stand was named after a famous battle that took place in 1900 during the Boer War. It was a terrible defeat for the British army and in remembrance of those that died some football stands around the country, such as those at Liverpool's Anfield stadium and Sheffield United's Bramall Lane, were named after the battle.

The Racecourse Ground was owned by Glyndwr University, who had taken it over when the previous owners had got into financial difficulties. Buying the ground was not an easy matter though. For starters, it was going to cost around £2 million. Rebuilding the Kop stand was going to cost a lot more.

The board needed the support of the members to make a bid. Of course, the members were fully behind the board's ambitious plan. Redeveloping the ground would be part of a big redevelopment of not just the stadium, but the whole area of Wrexham, including the nearby train station. The dream was to welcome international football to the Racecourse Ground – just as it had in the past. A new Kop stand would increase the capacity of the ground and make this dream more likely to come true.

Oddly, there was also an important visitor from the Canadian government! Ryan Reynolds was, of course, a Canadian, so when the Canadian Minister for International Development heard about him taking over Wrexham, he popped in to see what Ryan had bought. The minister was on his way to a meeting of the world's richest countries. He was obviously impressed with what he saw at the Racecourse as he wore a Wrexham face mask at the meeting! These were weird and wonderful times to be a Wrexham fan.

There were plans and improvements on the playing side, too. There was a new manager appointed for Wrexham's women's side and further additions to the men's team. Wrexham managed to snare themselves another top striker to partner Paul: Ollie Palmer, who became the club's record signing, costing £300,000 from AFC Wimbledon. He was a tall, powerful striker who had been grabbing goals and terrorizing defenders in various leagues for eight seasons. His height, experience and eye for goal were going to be a great help to Wrexham's promotion push.

Ollie was joined by reinforcements across the team. Callum McFadzean, a pacy wing-back, joined from Crewe Alexandria, and the under-21 Irish international defensive midfielder Thomas O'Connor, joined from Burton Albion. Both players could operate in more than one position, so gave Phil lots of options and cover when picking his match-day team. Finally, the goalkeeper Lee Camp joined as extra backup following an injury to the Wrexham number one, Rob

Lainton. They were strengthening the side at just the right time, ready for the second half of the season.

2022 started with a draw against their old rivals Notts County, but rather than knocking Wrexham off their stride, it seemed to make them more determined. Wrexham hit the new year like a train. Between 22nd January and 30th April Wrexham took an amazing 45 points from a possible 57, putting them right in the fight for the automatic promotion spot, and earning Phil the Manager of the Month Award for March.

Could this be Wrexham's season?

CHAPTER 12

WE FIGHT ON

8 May 2022, Racecourse Ground

There was one major obstacle to automatic promotion this season and it wasn't Wrexham's old foes Notts County this time. No, this season Stockport County had dominated the National League. By May they had been top of the table for three and a half months and had already beaten Wrexham at their ground. Wrexham were looking for revenge, but Stockport were looking for promotion – a win today would see County clinch top spot with two games to spare.

"Right lads," said Phil before the game, "we know Stockport can be beaten, they've lost two of their last three games. I reckon they're getting nervous. Don't let them settle on the ball – if you let them play they'll punish us. Keep it tight and get the ball in from the wings to Ollie and Paul. Right, let's go!"

"Yes Boss!" the team shouted as they headed for the pitch.

Keeping a team of Stockport's quality quiet was easier said than done. If they were nervous, they were doing a good job of hiding it. County took control of the early stages of the game. Their long-range passing was slick and accurate, and they had several chances to go ahead. Fortunately, Wrexham's keeper, Christian Dibble, was in inspired form.

"That's it, Chris! Top keeping!" Ben shouted as Christian smothered an early shot from distance.

When Christian's defences did get breached, Wrexham's teenage defensive sensation Max Cleworth was there to mop up, Max's 16th minute headed clearance being the only thing keeping County from their opening goal.

Slowly but surely, Wrexham were growing into the game and began to exert their own control. A

trademark long Ben Tozer throw caused chaos in the
County box and their keeper had to punch the ball
away. It only travelled to the middle of the box though,
and waiting there was Wrexham's ace predator, Super
Paul Mullin himself. Paul had peeled away from the
defenders and gambled that the ball would end up
exactly where it did. He spun on the spot and sent
an athletic overhead kick to the far top corner. The
crowd rose in expectation, ready to celebrate another
world-class goal – but the County keeper managed to
fingertip the ball over the bar to safety.

"The old Tozer throw to Mullin nearly did the trick
again!" laughed Max.

The resulting corner was swung in, Max leapt,
and made good contact with the ball, sending it just
wide of the post.

OOOOOOOOHHHHHHHHHHHHHHH!!!

"That's it Max! Keep pressing!" Phil encouraged
from the sidelines as the young player jogged back into
position. "And stay focused!"

Phil was right to warn his players – County were
still dangerous on the break. Moments later the ball

had gone wide to County's right; Wrexham's defenders were stretched, and the ball was pinged through to Stockport's number nine, Paddy Madden, who was clear on the edge of the box. Remarkably, for a player of Madden's quality, he sent the ball wide to the left.

"What did I just tell you?" bellowed Phil.

The lucky escape seemed to spur Wrexham into action. Pressing again, they won a throw on their right mid-way into County's half. Ben took the ball and gave it the usual wipe with the ball boy's towel. He flung in another long throw into the box and Ollie Palmer was there this time to flick the header into the net!

GOOOOOAAAAAAAALLLLLLLL!!!!!

"It's not just you who can score from Ben's throws," laughed Ollie as he passed Paul.

"I'd better get on the scoresheet," grinned Paul. "I can't have you being top scorer!"

He didn't have long to wait. On the stroke of half time the ball was pinged over from midfield by Jordan Davies. County were playing a high defensive line, but Paul was lurking on the shoulder of the nearest defender. Paul reacted first and sprinted away with the ball, defenders trailing in his wake. The County keeper ran forward from his line, Paul glanced up – and rifled the ball into the bottom corner from the edge of the box!

GOOOOOAAAAAAAALLLLLLLL!!!!!

"Paul doesn't miss chances like that, Steve!" said Phil to his assistant. Phil might have looked stern, but inside he was overjoyed. Wrexham's deadly duo had put them 2–0 up against the league leaders. If Wrexham could see this result out, they would go top of the league themselves!

In fact, it went even better for Wrexham. Straight after the break Wrexham won a free kick mid-way into County's half, by the right touchline. The kick was swung in beautifully into the box where Ollie shrugged off the covering defender and planted a firm header past the Stockport keeper.

GOOOOOAAAAAAAALLLLLLLL!!!!!

The crowd were in dreamland! Ben nearly made it four at the end of the game, forcing a smart save down low from the County keeper, but it didn't really matter. Wrexham were in top spot in the National

League. Stockport had two games left, but Wrexham had only one. Their final game against Dagenham and Redbridge was a must-win – if Wrexham were victorious they could be champions!

CHAPTER 13

SO NEAR YET SO FAR

15 May 2022, Chigwell Construction Stadium

Stockport County won their game in hand to go three points clear of Wrexham. It all came down to this game. Stockport were now favourites for promotion, as all they had to do was avoid defeat in their final game, a tricky home tie against Halifax. Wrexham had to win their game at Dagenham and Redbridge and hope Halifax won against Stockport. Dagenham and Redbridge had an outside chance of making the play-offs, too, so it would be a tough match.

Wrexham would be well supported. They might have been playing away from home, but the away

end was sold out, with Wrexham fans eager to urge
their team on. They wanted to be there if this was the
moment Wrexham were promoted.

Phil tried to get the team ready as best he could
before the game. "Now remember," he said, "we gave
Stockport too much time and space last week and that
nearly came back to bite us on the backside. We can't
afford to do that today. I want you to play the game,
not the occasion. Over 90 minutes I back you to beat
this team any day of the week. Now go out there and
make me proud."

"Come on boys!" shouted Ben. "Let's
make this count!"

The early stages of the game were tight and
competitive. The Daggers, as Dagenham and
Redbridge were known, went close early on, but so
did Wrexham. Ben floated in a cross from the right
touchline and Paul trapped it mid-air with his back to
goal, spun athletically and struck the ball on the volley
– but the keeper saved. The away fans groaned – it
was a clever shot, but they needed goals. Then news
came filtering through – Stockport had gone 1–0 up!

"Someone's just said County are leading," said Ollie.

"Yeah, but we can't worry about that," said Ben. "We've just got to do what we can do. Let's get this game won."

However, the Daggers looked more likely to pinch a winner than Wrexham. A flying save from Christian was all that stopped Dagenham and Redbridge from going one up. Their strike force had a fistful of good attempts without finding the target; Wrexham replied with a shot from the edge of the box by Paul that looked like it had found the bottom corner but went agonisingly wide instead. There was also a rasping drive from Callum that went whistling over the bar, but the keeper had it covered anyway.

Things appeared to get worse in the 35th minute when Daggers striker Paul McCallum thought he'd finally found the net, but the goal was ruled out for a foul on Christian. The Daggers were finding it too easy to pass through Wrexham's lines, and the defence found itself facing wave after wave of attacks. They did well to restrict the opposition to shooting from range, though Wrexham were lucky that they seemed to have left their scoring boots in the changing room. When they did get their shots on target, Christian was there to keep his side in the game with two more excellent blocks – one down low with his right boot and a full-length save down low to his right.

"Blinding saves, Christian," said Ben as they trudged off the field at half time.

"Thanks," he replied. "Hard work today isn't it?"

"You're telling me – we've got it all to do in the second half!"

Wrexham started the second half with renewed purpose. Ollie found space in the box and fired in a shot, but it was straight at the keeper!

"I should have done better with that!" muttered Ollie under his breath.

It felt like things just weren't going Wrexham's way. That feeling was confirmed when news came through that Stockport had gone 2–0 up! It would take a miracle now for Wrexham to go top. The news seemed to deflate Wrexham; a sloppy clearance put Daggers on the attack, and the defence switched off, allowing an attacker time in the box to shoot past Christian and take the lead! Things were going from bad to worse!

Ollie had a chance to pull a goal back as he burst past the last defender, but a poor touch pushed the ball too far forward and the keeper claimed it. Ollie threw his head back and howled in frustration.

Daggers were piling on the pressure and more spaces appeared when Wrexham tried to force an equalizer. Another flying stop from Christian kept Wrexham in it, but eventually the pressure told when Daggers doubled the lead with a header from a well-worked corner routine.

Chances came and went for both sides, but the game was finally put to bed when Daggers put a third past a tired-looking Wrexham side in the 90th minute. Wrexham had failed. There were to be no miracles today. So near, yet so far.

"Okay, we've not got top spot," said Phil to his disappointed team in the changing room. "Today was not our day; but we've got the next best thing in second place. That takes us straight into the play-off semi-final and give us home advantage. I just want to say I'm really proud of the way you've played these last few weeks. Let's make it count. It's all big games from now on boys!"

He was right. The next game for Wrexham wasn't the play-offs, but a trip to Wembley! During Wrexham's excellent run of form, they'd also been working through the rounds of the FA Trophy, the competition for clubs from the National League and below. Wrexham had played excellently in the previous five rounds, beating tough sides such as Notts County and the new champions Stockport County. Now it was the time for the final against fellow National League side Bromley. Wrexham had drawn with Bromley away from home and had beaten them at the Racecourse, so were feeling confident. They may not have won the league, but promotion and a trophy were still within their grasp.

CHAPTER 14

WEMBLEY!

May 22, 2022, Wembley Stadium

The Wrexham team coach pulled into Wembley Way
on the way to drop the players outside the changing
rooms. Even though some of the players had been here
before, the magic of the stadium got to all of them.
The iconic arch loomed above them.

"This is what it's all about," said Paul, gazing up at
the world-famous structure.

"We could be back here in a couple of weeks, for
the play-off final," said Christian.

"Don't count your chickens before they hatch," Ben
chided, good naturedly. "Let's just concentrate on one

game at a time, shall we?"

With a hiss of brakes, the bus came to a slow halt outside the entrance that led to the changing rooms. Phil stood at the front of the bus as the players got ready to get off.

"Right boys – let's go make some memories!" he said with a smile. The door swung open, and he led them off into the stadium and their date with destiny.

The players weren't the only ones with butterflies going into Wembley. A visit to the home of English football with the possibility of picking up silverware had been too big an occasion for owners Rob and Ryan to miss out on. They'd found a gap in their filming, producing and writing schedules to make the jump over the Atlantic for the match, and their families came too. They'd invited some of their celebrity friends as well, with the comedy actor and performer Will Ferrell and footballing legend David Beckham joining the owners in their private box for the game.

To the side of them, the Wrexham fans were in good voice and in high spirits. They'd travelled down to Wembley in their thousands and were hoping for a triumphant end to their season.

It was an energetic start to the game from both teams. Ollie flicked a ball down the right for Paul, who raced onto the ball and surged deep into the box. It looked like he was boxed in by the defender near the touchline, but he magically cut the ball back into the centre of the box, right into the path of Ollie. A first time shot! But it cannoned into the defender and rebounded to safety. Close! A warning for Bromley.

A short while later Paul was again playing the role of provider. This time the ball was fired down the right, where Paul's pace got him past the first defender. Unfortunately, there were *three* defenders ready to surround him – even Paul couldn't play round all of them! It looked like the attack had fizzled into nothing, but Paul fired the ball across the box for a sprinting Jordan Davies to latch onto. He didn't quite catch the ball sweetly enough and it lacked the power to trouble the Bromley keeper.

Jordan span away in frustration but clapped his hands to acknowledge the beautifully timed pass.

"Great ball, Paul!" he shouted with a thumbs up.

"Just stick it in the net next time," Paul joked with a wry smile.

It wasn't one way traffic for Wrexham, though – Bromley hadn't got to the final by accident and were a decent footballing side. They proved that when Harry Forster curled a dangerous ball over the bar.

"OOOOOOHHHHHHH!" gasped the Wrexham fans.

The first half ended goalless. It was too close to call how this one would go.

"Let's make this count, boys!" Ben shouted as he led them from the tunnel and onto the pitch for the second half.

With Ben leading by example, Wrexham began the second half with more urgency. Ben bombarded the box with his special long throws. Jordan put one just wide and another was cleared by the defence. Just as it seemed Wrexham were on top, Christian was quickly called into action to thwart two Bromley attacks, saving dangerous shots from their top scorer Michael Cheek.

The action was going from one end to the other. A

slick Wrexham move led to the ball finding Paul free on the left-hand side of the box. With time to steady himself Paul shot with his favoured left foot, but the angle was against him, and he fired the ball into the side netting. On the sidelines Phil was beginning to get concerned.

"We need to start taking these chances," he muttered under his breath.

He was right to be worried – a long ball from the Bromley half landed perfectly for Bromley's Corey Whitely. His run into the box dragged in two Wrexham defenders, leaving Michael Cheek free in acres of space. Christian charged forward to close down the angle, but instead of shooting Whitely threaded the ball between the defenders to the unmarked Cheek, who hammered the ball into the empty net. Bromley had broken the deadlock!

"GOOOOOOAAAALLLLL!" screamed the Bromley fans.

"Heads up lads," shouted Phil as they lined up again for the restart. "There's still half an hour to play – plenty of time to get back into this!"

Wrexham weren't going to let their manager – never mind their fans – down. They surged forward seeking an equalizer. David Jones fed the ball to Jordan, who scampered to the goal line and flashed a ball across the mouth of the goal. Unfortunately, there wasn't a Wrexham shirt anywhere near it to take advantage. Another long throw from Ben fell to Jake Hyde, whose goal-bound header was tipped over the bar by the Bromley keeper. Jake had another chance moments later as Jordan fed a beautiful ball into the box from the right touchline, but the bounce was unkind and went wide. Time was running out. Wrexham were piling on the pressure – surely a goal had to come!

Wrexham were finding some joy on the right. As the final seconds drew near Paul tried his luck and went on a surging run down the touchline, gliding past the Bromley defence. He fired in a cross, the ball ricocheted around – then Jake was there to head it home!

"GOOOOOOOAAAAAAALLLLLLLLL!" The Wrexham fans exploded with joy.

But their joy was short-lived – the assistant referee

had their flag up for off-side! The celebrations stopped – apart from in the owners' box where Rob and Ryan had been too busy celebrating to see the flag. David Beckham had, of course, and had to break the bad news to the happy owners.

The decision knocked the last of the belief out of Wrexham and moments later the whistle blew. The game was over. Wrexham were left empty-handed.

Two important games and two losses. There was still another important game to come, though. The Red Dragons needed to dust themselves down and go straight back into battle.

CHAPTER 15

THE GAME OF THE SEASON

28 May 2022 Racecourse Ground

The home changing room of the Racecourse Ground had seen plenty of celebrations this season, but the atmosphere was tense as the players waited for the game to begin. The play-off semi-final. Win this and they were back to Wembley for the play-off final. Lose and the season that had promised so much was over with nothing to show for it but a loser's medal from the FA Trophy. Lots of memories, but bitter ones from when it mattered.

"We all know what happened last week," said Phil. The players didn't need reminding. "But we played well – remember that. All we lacked was that little bit of quality in the final third, that killer ball. That game's history now and when it's all said and done it was a sideshow – a nice distraction. When we started the season, the aim was to get promotion and that's still our goal. We can't let that last game throw us off our stride. We've earned the right to play this game at home. Grimsby did well to knock out Notts County, but we've got a great record here – let's make this count."

Nearly 10,000 fans were crammed into the Racecourse Ground for the game and were in good voice as the game kicked off. However, it was Grimsby who burst into action. In a shock for the home fans, Grimsby's John McAtee had the ball in Wrexham's net – however the assistant referee's flag saved the home side. McAtee had been *just* off-side.

Following that early scare, Wrexham began to take control of the game.

"We've got Mullin, super Paul Mullin…" The words of the now famous chant rolled around the Racecourse. And it was super Paul who struck the first blow. Charging into the Grimsby box he was brought down by the Grimsby skipper, Luke Waterfall. The referee had no hesitation in blowing for a penalty. The fans went wild.

"Looked a bit soft to me," Ben muttered to Ollie.

"Yeah, but I'm not complaining," smiled Ollie.

Paul settled the ball on the spot, took a few steps back and waited for the whistle. The ref put the whistle to his lips and blew. Paul ran forward and smashed a cannonball of a shot into the roof of the net.

Paul peeled away and was mobbed by his teammates.

"I don't care who the keeper is – no one was saving that!" screamed Jordan.

Their joy was short-lived though. A couple of minutes later Grimsby poured forward in numbers. The ball fell to McAtee, just outside the box. There was no stopping him this time though, and he curled a beautiful strike past Christian.

GOOOOOOOAAAAAALLLLLLLLLL!

It was the travelling support celebrating this time.

Wrexham weren't going to be knocked back, though. Bryce Hosannah tried to replicate McAtee's strike, but his well-struck shot was saved by the Grimsby goalie. The keeper had no chance with Paul's header a couple of minutes later, though. The classic combination of a long throw into the box and Paul's deadly finishing led to Wrexham's leading scorer heading firmly into the goal, despite the close attention of a Wrexham defender.

"GOOOOOOAAAAA..."

The cheer died in the throats of the home fans before it could even get going. The referee had blown for a foul.

"Ref! What was that for?" shouted Paul, arms outstretched.

The referee wasn't going to change his mind, of course. As far as he was concerned, he'd seen a foul and that was that.

It nearly didn't matter. Ollie crossed the ball in from the right to Jordan, who crossed it into the middle of the box, where Paul tried an acrobatic overhead kick. It ended up being an air shot, but it didn't matter because the ball fell for Bryce, a couple of yards out. He went for the header and was cleaned out by the Grimsby keeper!

"Penalty!" screamed the fans, but the referee waved play on!

"You don't know what you're doing! You don't know what you're doing!" chanted the fans.

Wrexham were building the pressure. Yet another long throw from Ben caused so much confusion in the box that the ball smashed off the back of a Grimsby defender's head, and it was only a world-class save that stopped Wrexham taking the lead. Jordan then saw one of his headers cleared off the line with the keeper beaten – it was all Wrexham. However, just like Wembley, they couldn't put the chances away – and the half finished with scores tied 1–1.

CHAPTER 16

IT NEVER RAINS...

28 May 2022 Racecourse Ground

The second half kicked off and it was Grimsby who set
the early pace. The fans barely had chance to get back
to their seats before Christian had to save another
McAtee effort and another from Harry Clifton, which
he pushed out for a corner. Christian punched away
the resulting kick from just under his bar, but then the
ball was swung back in, and Grimsby's skipper headed
the ball home. Grimsby had taken the lead, 2–1! Apart
from the celebrating away fans, the Racecourse was
stunned into silence!

If it wasn't for two more top-drawer saves by

Christian, it would have been a whole lot worse for Wrexham. This was not how the game was meant to go. Luke Young, Wrexham's captain, tried his best to rally his team.

"Come on Wrexham! Let's tighten this up!" he bellowed.

Luke's words had the desired effect – Wrexham went on the attack. They won a corner which was floated to the edge of the six-yard box. Ben was there and powered a header home!

GOOOOOAAAAAALLLLLLLL!!!!!!

Ben Tozer was involved in a goal again but this time he was the scorer and not providing the assist. Wrexham were level.

Barely two minutes later and Ben was in action again – this time in his more traditional role of hurling dangerous balls into the box from the sidelines. His long throw fell to Ollie, who cleverly flicked the ball to the far post where his strike partner was lurking. Paul was never one to turn down an opportunity like that, and he duly squeezed his header between the keeper and the post.

GOOOOOAAAAAALLLLLLLL!!!!!!

Wrexham had gone back into the lead – the semi-final was end-to-end entertainment. Now it was the Wrexham's fans turn to sing and celebrate.

It wasn't to last. Five minutes later the ever-dangerous McAtee picked up the ball near the edge of the box and curled an inch-perfect cross for Ryan Taylor, who dived in front of the last Wrexham defender and scored with a first-time header for Grimsby. The Mariners had drawn level again! The score was now 3–3 and the Wrexham fans were stunned into silence. Surely they weren't going to let victory slip through their fingers again?

It got worse. A run-of-the-mill corner was floated in to the far post where an unmarked Emmanuel Dieseruvwe had all the space in the world to put Grimsby back into the lead. On the sidelines Phil was a ball of frustration.

"Come on boys!" he shouted. "We've got to get the basics right!"

The crowd, sensing their team needed lifting, spurred them on. Paul picked up the ball to the right of midfield and turned on the afterburners. He powered to the edge of the box and struck a fierce shot. It was destined for the top corner, but the Grimsby keeper clawed it away and behind. This roused the crowd into even louder cheering, the noise like a wave, rolling around the historic old ground.

Now it was Wrexham's turn to try floating a corner into the danger zone. This time the ball drifted to the far corner of the six-yard box where Jordan leapt higher than the defender and headed into the top of the net!

GOOOOOAAAAAALLLLLLLL!!!!!!

It was 4–4 with ten minutes to play. It was anyone's guess how this would play out.

Five minutes later, Ollie picked up the ball in the middle of the park. He looked to lay it off to Paul, but he was too well marked. Instead, he twisted and turned on a diagonal run across the pitch, Grimsby players nipping at his heels. Ollie picked out Callum McFadzean who was overlapping on his left. Callum crossed a dangerous ball into the middle of the box, where a Grimsby defender managed to head the ball clear. However, the ball fell straight to Jordan, who fired the ball straight back towards goal. His left foot volley dipped over the keeper's despairing jump ... but cleared the bar too. The fans groaned with disappointment.

Next it was Callum's turn to test the keeper. Linking up with Jordan he shimmied past a pair of defenders and fired in a rasping drive that the keeper did well to palm away. Wrexham were dominating the latter stages of the game for sure! But just as it looked like there could be only one winner, Grimsby took a long throw from the Wrexham left. The ball arced into the box, but in the crush of attackers and defenders the ball went out for a goal kick. It was too close for comfort though! The referee blew his whistle – it was going to be extra-time!

"I don't know about you, Paul, but I'm shattered," muttered Ollie as they lined up for the kick-off of the first period of extra time.

"You're telling me," he replied. "This had better not go to penalties."

The referee blew his whistle and the game resumed.

It was tense – the players were tiring and were scared of making the mistake that would cost their team the game. Chances were few and far between. Jordan went down in the box in a tangle of legs, but the referee wasn't interested in awarding a penalty for what looked like a coming together of two players.

The first half of extra time came and went. The second half was similarly devoid of excitement, and the clock ticked down to what felt like the inevitable penalties. Phil had tried to freshen things up to force an equalizer, even replacing the tiring Ollie with Jake, but Wrexham couldn't find the decisive goal.

As the game drifted to a close, Grimsby took a throw deep into Wrexham territory. The ball looked nothing special, but it fell kindly to the Mariner captain Luke Waterfall who made a great connection with his head and powered the ball past Christian's desperate dive and into the bottom corner. Grimsby had grabbed a winner in the last seconds of the game!

Wrexham looked shell-shocked. They seemed to be almost in a daze as they played out the last moments of the game. The referee's whistle went. The game was over. Grimsby had won 5–4 and were into the play-off final.

Wrexham's season was over. In the last three games they had lost the chance of automatic promotion, a Wembley final, and a play-off semi-final. It was true what they say – it never rains, but it pours. Wrexham would be in the National League for another season.

CHAPTER 17

A PHOENIX FROM THE FLAMES

6 August 2022, Racecourse Ground

Myths from different countries tell tales of the phoenix. This mythical bird does something extraordinary when it dies – it bursts into flames, and out of the fire a new phoenix is born. Those people who saw the result of Wrexham's titanic match against Grimsby in the semi-final might have expected the last-gasp winner for the Mariners to take some getting over – but they would have been wrong. Out of the fires of defeat, something magical happened in North Wales, too. A new belief and hunger for success was born.

It started the moment the final whistle was blown. Instead of trudging miserably home, the Wrexham fans stayed, and they sang. They sang like the crowds had done in the glory days, they sang as if they had won the league, rather than lost a play-off. They sang like they *believed*.

That renewed belief was coursing through the veins of one of the owners, Ryan, who was watching on. He knew that the next season had to be the one. Spending fifteen seasons in non-league football was way too long for a club like Wrexham. He'd spent a lot of money, and he knew there would be a lot more spending to come. This preseason was all important – Wrexham had to be the phoenix from the flames.

The belief was in Phil, too. He'd worked at a lot of clubs as either a player or a manager, and he could see that something special was happening at Wrexham. He could see how the success that was building on the pitch was being reflected outside. There was a buzz around the club and a buzz around the town. Having rich, celebrity owners helped, for sure, and it certainly attracted the day-trippers and sightseers. They brought extra money into the club, and the town, too.

Next season had to be the one to keep that momentum going. The squad needed building – adding that little bit of quality that would make the difference. It would cost, of course, but you couldn't just buy the league – it would also take coaching, care and a bit of luck.

Preseason, that time of training and tweaking ideas, squads and formations, went well for Wrexham. Phil, just as he'd planned, added some excellent players to the squad. Midfielders Elliot Lee and Anthony Forde added some Football League experience, as did the Carlisle United goalkeeper, Mark Howard. Mark was brought in as both Christian and first-choice keeper Rob Lainton were suffering from the effects of long-term injuries. Phil also brought in Jordan Tunnicliffe from League Two side Crawley Town to help stiffen up the defence.

These new players did not come cheap. Wrexham were outspending their National League rivals. The new players were on Football League wages, too, meaning Wrexham's wage bill was the highest in the

National League. And this wasn't the only expenditure happening during the close season. The old, derelict Kop stand was finally being demolished to make way for a new state-of-the-art stand. Things were happening on and off the pitch – it was just as well those famous owners had deep pockets!

Their smart transfer business and strong preseason results made Wrexham the favourites to nab promotion in most pundits' opinions. However, it wasn't to be taken for granted – there were some very good teams in the National League this year. Chesterfield were looking dangerous and were also heavily backed to go up. There were also their old rivals Notts County. They too were desperate to seal promotion, also feeling the National League was beneath a club of their history and pedigree. That one automatic promotion place was going to be keenly contested this season!

Wrexham's first chance to see if their preseason form would continue into the league season came on 6th August when they opened their league campaign at home to Eastleigh. Wrexham knew all about the

Spitfires from previous seasons and it would be a good test of how far they had come. The Racecourse Ground was rocking with expectant fans. They believed this was going to be their season, but would belief become reality?

Luke Young was captain this season for Wrexham. He looked around the changing room as the team prepared to take the pitch. Mark – making his full debut in goal – was joking with Elliot, who was on the bench. Paul and Ollie were making bets as to who would score more goals. Would they beat their combined total of 37 goals from last season? Luke hoped so. What wasn't up for debate was that the team spirit was good.

Luke got his teammates' attention. "We've done well preseason, but that counts for nothing when we cross that white line," he said. "We're going to be judged by what we do when it matters. We've got the quality – let's make it happen!"

The boys cheered and clattered out. Phil nodded gravely as they went.

"It's got to be this season," he said to Steve, his

assistant. "We can't afford another year in this division. If we don't go up this time it'll be a disaster."

"Don't worry boss – I can feel it in my bones. We're doing it this year!" said Steve.

"Well, I hope those bones are right! For all our sakes," Phil replied with a wry smile as they followed their players onto the pitch.

The game, typically for a season opener, was a cagey affair, with both sides cautiously testing each other, and some early-season nerves on display. These nerves might explain what happened next. Eastleigh had a throw-in deep in the Wrexham half. The Spitfires player threw a long, looping ball into the box. It was high and slow, and Mark was right underneath it, but rather than catch it or punch it clear he ended up scooping it weakly a couple of feet behind him. The ball dropped right in front of an Eastleigh player who tapped it home into an empty net. Eastleigh were ahead!

No one could quite believe what they had seen. This certainly wasn't what anyone expected!

"Focus!" screamed Phil from the technical area.

Wrexham were sparked into life.

Paul headed over, under pressure from the Eastleigh defence. Mark redeemed himself with a sliding save with the attacker clean through. Ollie headed wide in a crowded box and then saw a shot flash wide of the left post. Jordan saw his shot go wide too. But Wrexham finished the half a goal down.

Eastleigh started the new half brightly with Mark forced into a smart stop at the base of his right post. Elliot was subbed on and suddenly his fancy footwork had an instant impact. He slipped the ball through a crowded midfield to release Paul, whose shot went just wide.

"That's it, Elliot!" shouted Phil.

Wrexham were building the pressure. Elliot dipped his shoulder and made space for himself on the edge of the box. He fired in a shot that was blocked away – but it was clear that he was going to be a player to watch. Moments later Elliot had the ball on the left of the area. He danced one way then another before sending in a pinpoint pass to Ollie, who headed over.

"Keep them coming!" Paul shouted to Elliot – he

knew service like that would lead to a hatful of goals.

A couple of minutes later and the roles were reversed – Ollie cleverly back-heeled the ball to Elliot, who hammered home.

GOOOOOAAAAALLLLLLLL!!!!!!!

Wrexham were back in it.

Next it was Paul's turn to get an assist, bringing the ball under control before slipping the ball to Elliot who crashed the ball home again for the Wrexham winner!

GOOOOOAAAAALLLLLLLL!!!!!!!

The fans and players celebrated in the August sunshine. Elliot had bagged a brace on his debut and Wrexham were on their way!

CHAPTER 18

BATTLE OF THE GOAL MACHINES

4 October 2022, Meadow Lane

"We are top of the league, say we are top of the league. We are top of the league, say we are top of the league," chanted the Wrexham fans as they made their way into Meadow Lane, home of their closest rivals, Notts County.

Both sides had been sweeping the opposition away this season. Wrexham had been scoring for fun. So far, they had beaten both Maidstone United and Dorking 5–0, Dagenham and Redbridge 4–1, and had put six past Torquay United without reply. Three days earlier they had beaten Oldham Athletic 2–1 away from home to go top of the National League.

Wrexham were on an eight-game unbeaten run, but that evening though they were up against their toughest opponents – Notts County. The Magpies couldn't match Wrexham for financial muscle, but they could more than hold their own on the history front, as the oldest team in the world. They may have been languishing in non-league football now, but up front they had one of the National League's most lethal forwards – Macaulay Langstaff.

Langstaff had burst onto the scene the season before when his goals had helped National League North side Gateshead to promotion to the National League. Now he was playing for the Magpies and was terrorizing defences up and down the country. Wrexham knew that they would have their hands full try to contain him.

"It's all well and good trying to mark Langstaff out of the game," said Phil as he addressed the team before the game, "but remember they've got other dangerous players, too. We can't give them space or they'll hurt us. We know them and they know us.

"They play with a high line, so if we time our runs right, we're in. We've worked hard to get to the top, but make no mistake, we're going to have to fight even harder to stay there tonight."

The referee blew his whistle and both teams immediately started slugging it out, trying to get the upper hand. Being the home side, with the crowd roaring them on, the Magpies took the early initiative and were attacking Wrexham from one flank and then the other. They won a free kick in a dangerous position near the Wrexham area. Rather than fire the free kick towards goal, County played the ball out wide, and a couple of intricate passes later the ball came to Langstaff, unmarked, virtually on the penalty spot. He lashed the ball home like he had done so many times already that season. 1–0 to County.

Ollie nearly got the equalizer, but the Wrexham striker shot wide. Mark and the Wrexham defenders were being kept busy by wave after wave of County attacks. The Magpies were good value for their lead and Mark had to save another Langstaff shot in injury time.

In the second half Wrexham took the fight back to Notts County. Ollie had another shot, but the Magpies' keeper was equal to it.

"That's it, Ollie," Luke shouted. "Keep at them!"

Paul wasn't managing to get any space to get a clear shot away, but he could turn provider. He slipped a ball into the path of James Jones, who blasted the ball into the net!

GOOOOOAAAAALLLLLLL!!!!!!

Nearly 2,000 Wrexham fans who had made the long journey leapt into the air, but – oh no! The assistant referee had their flag up for offside.

The game swung one way then another, but there was no way in for either team – good defending and poor finishing meant no one could add to the scoreline. The game finished 1–0 to County. Not only had they won the game, they had also leapfrogged Wrexham to go into top spot. Notts County were leading the National League.

The away dressing room was not a happy place. Phil looked around at his dejected players.

"We deserved a point," he said, "but we weren't

ruthless enough in front of goal. We've scored a lot of goals this season and we'll score a lot more, but it's been one of those nights. Any other day we score from those chances and if we got one, I'm sure we would have got another."

Phil pointed in the direction of the home dressing room. "They'll be celebrating in there, because they know they got away with it tonight. But this is going to be a long hard season. We've got to be cool, calm and collected because we've got another game on Saturday. Let's look forward to it."

CHAPTER 19

BACK TO WINNING WAYS

8 October 2022, Racecourse Ground

Steve walked into Phil's office at the training ground holding a sheet of paper.

"Do you want the good news or bad news on Jordan's injury?" he asked.

Jordan Davies had been substituted during the Notts County game after taking a knock.

"Give me the good news first," said Phil.

"His injury isn't as bad as I feared," replied Steve.

"Okay that is good news," said Phil. "So what's the bad news?"

"He'll probably not be fit for Saturday," said Steve.

Phil grimaced. "Hmm, not good news. We'll take a late call on that one to give him every chance to get right. He's an important player for us. If he's not, maybe this is the time to give Elliot his start."

Out on the practise pitch the Wrexham players were going through their paces. They were doing attack versus defence drills, and Elliot was on the ball. He dropped his shoulder to glide past Aaron Hayden before pinging an inch-perfect pass to Paul's feet. The star striker hit a crisp low shot into the bottom corner.

"Nice work Super Sub!" he said with a smile, giving a thumbs up.

Elliot laughed – it was true, he had been something of a wizard from the bench and was already a fans' favourite. And it was nice that he had settled so quickly into his new team. However, the laugh hid a growing sense of frustration. The fact he wasn't starting was beginning to get on his nerves. He was playing well when he got the chance, so what more could he do to get more game time? Maybe he needed to speak to the boss – let Phil know he wasn't happy. In the meantime, there was training to focus on.

"Hey dreamer! You've just been 'megged by a centre half and you didn't even notice!" shouted Ollie.

Elliot laughed again and went to chase down the ball. He might be frustrated, but he knew his time would come.

Mad. There was no other word for it. It was the craziest game. Jordan had failed his late fitness test, so Elliot had come into the team and to begin with Wrexham were all over Barnet. Aaron Hayden had put them in the lead and Barnet looked in danger of receiving a good old-fashioned hiding. Then, amazingly, Barnet pulled a goal back and then went into the lead. Fortunately, goals from Tom O'Connor and Paul had put Wrexham back in the lead by half time and it felt that the Welsh fans could relax a bit. Wrexham had this in the bag.

Someone forgot to tell that to Barnet though. The second half was hardly underway and Barnet had equalized again. Phil's words from half time drifted into Luke's head:

"Don't underestimate Barnet. They had a good win

in their last game and they'll fancy this."

"Come on boys!" Luke bellowed, "Let's get a grip on this!"

The players were in no mood to let more points slip through their fingers. They went on a goal bonanza! Paul – who else – got them level!

GOOOOOAAALLLLLL!!!!

Luke, leading by example, put them ahead.

GOOOOOAAALLLLLL!!!!

Aaron got his second of the game, too.

GOOOOOAAALLLLLL!!!!

And finally, after a world-class pass from Elliot, Ollie tucked another one away for the Red Dragons.

GOOOOOAAALLLLLL!!!!

Wrexham had scored four goals in 11 minutes! They were 7–3 up and cruising!

If the Wrexham fans were dreaming about scoring more, then Barnet were about to give them a rude awakening. In the 75th minute a Barnet attacker got in front of the covering defender and finished past Mark to pull a goal back. A few minutes later they scored again to make it 7–5! Surely there couldn't be a comeback? The Wrexham fans started to have little niggles of doubt. They had wanted a hatful of goals, but now they sound of the final whistle started to get more appealing. The groans of the supporters when the board went up showing seven minutes of extra time told its own story.

Ollie had a chance to claim a second goal, but he headed over - then disaster! A mix-up between Aaron and Ben and let in Barnet attacker Nicke Kabamba again! He'd already scored twice for the North London side and was dreaming of his hat-trick – but Mark was there to save the day, with the save of the game.

"What a stop!" shouted Aaron – the idea of his mistake making it 7–6 didn't bear thinking about.

He needn't have worried though; that was the end of the scoring. Wrexham had won a 12-goal thriller – the most goals scored in a single match at the Racecourse since 1934. Absolutely mad.

Although Wrexham's defence had let them down at times during the game, the important point was they were back to winning ways. It was a feeling they wanted to hang on to – and Wrexham went on an amazing run. They won seven of their next ten games, drawing the remaining three. By the close of the year, Wrexham and their arch-rivals, Notts County, were proving they were the form teams of the division. They were neck and neck, and no one could call how the second half of the season would pan out.

They were in for a treat...

CHAPTER 20

GUESS WHO'S BACK

25 March 2023, Racecourse Ground

New Year's Day. The weak, watery light of January broke over the venerable old Racecourse Ground. The Red Dragons had finished the old year in a run of unbelievable form. Normally such a run would have seen them well clear at the top of the league, but not this season. This time another team was performing just as well.

Notts County – just as desperate to taste proper League football again – were matching Wrexham point for point. Wrexham had a marginally better home record; County had a slightly better away record. The question supporters of both teams were asking was who would blink first? Which team would keep their form going into the new year?

Wrexham were doing their best to make sure it was them who would finish in top spot. They burst into the second half of the season with the same ruthless drive that they had shown before Christmas. The Red Dragons went through all of January and February unbeaten, winning ten out of their eleven games, only dropping points in a 2–2 home draw with Woking.

The team was looking settled and were running smoothly. The defence, with first-choice keeper Rob Lainton between the posts, was proving difficult to beat. Up front, the deadly duo of Paul and Ollie were hammering in the goals on a regular basis. Wrexham were scoring more than twice the goals they were conceding. In those first 11 games Wrexham had scored an incredible 29 goals while only conceding 13. That was league-winning form.

March started with a rare draw before normal service was resumed with wins against Dagenham and Redbridge and Southend. It was beginning to feel like there was nothing the other teams in the division could do stop the runaway train that was Wrexham. But just as it looked like things were getting too easy, fate intervened.

Wrexham were playing away at Bromley's Hayes Lane ground. Unlucky not to have gone ahead early in the first half, Wrexham were having to weather a bit of Bromley pressure as the half went on. The game was drifting towards the break when Rob grimaced as the ball was cleared upfield.

"You alright mate?" asked Ben, concerned that his friend might be in trouble.

"Yeah, I think so. Feels like I've done something to my knee. I'll probably be able to run it off," Rob replied, though he didn't look convinced.

When the teams came back out for the second half, it was Mark between the sticks, not Rob, as he was unable to continue. Fortunately, a couple of goals from Paul ensured that Wrexham came back from their trip to Kent with three points.

Even better, their deadly rivals Notts County had dropped more points, drawing their second game on the trot. Wrexham were now three points ahead of the Magpies with a game in hand. However, the injury to Rob dampened the celebrations.

Unfortunately, Rob's injury was worse than anyone had feared. He had damaged his knee ligaments and the club doctor reckoned he would be ruled out for the next six weeks. That was a blow – not just for Rob, but for the team. Their back-up, Mark, was an experienced keeper, but he had gone down with a long-term injury too. The squad was looking very light with both Rob and Mark on the sidelines. Wrexham needed reinforcements and they needed them quickly.

And did they ever get someone! The Red Dragons had a decent sprinkling of players with actual league know-how: both Paul and Ollie were experienced lower-league players, and Ben Tozer had played at Championship level. Better still, Eoghan O'Connell had been with Celtic in the Scottish Premiership and had even played against the mighty Barcelona in the Champions League.

But when an actual England international walked into the club, it wasn't just the Wrexham players and supporters that were surprised – football supporters across the country sat up and took notice.

Ben Foster had played 390 games in the Premier League for four different clubs, including Manchester United, as well as over 100 games for other clubs. He had also been capped for England, playing eight games for his national team. He was also, importantly, a trophy winner with Wrexham! Early in his career he had been loaned to the Red Dragons and was between the posts when they won the Football League Trophy in 2005. Ben went from his loan spell to have a glittering career, while Wrexham had slipped quietly out of the league. Now he was back.

Ben had actually retired from football at the end of the previous season, so when he got a call from Ryan Reynolds he was as surprised as anyone. Ryan talked to Ben about coming out of retirement to sign a short-term deal until the end of the season to help Wrexham's push for promotion. In truth Ben hadn't needed much persuading. As he told a disbelieving media:

"I would have only come out of retirement for

Wrexham – genuinely only for Wrexham. I know the club and I owe them so much. They gave me that springboard to start my career and show what I could do. And then I got my run at Manchester United – so it all started here."

Ben wasn't match-fit, and he didn't have the luxury of a preseason to get into shape – but he had a game to play.

The visitors to the Racecourse that day were York City. The Minstermen had struggled that season – dangerous in front of goal, but leaky at the back. A tricky side, but the packed Racecourse was expecting a win and were in the mood to celebrate. The Hollywood stardust of their owners had brought Ben Foster back to them, and they wanted to give him a second debut to remember – a full eighteen years after his first appearance.

It was just the kind of game Ben would have wanted, too. Wrexham dominated the first half, with Paul and Ollie dragging the defence around, allowing the Red Dragons' midfield of Elliot and Luke to run rings around the opposition.

In the 42nd minute the pressure finally told when James Jones smashed a shot against the Minstermen's crossbar which then rebounded off the keeper and rolled in: one-nil up at the break and looking comfortable. The second half followed the same pattern and when Wrexham put two more past the York keeper it was game over. Wrexham stayed top.

Notts County were still at their shoulder though, matching them point for point. Wrexham smashed Oldham Athletic 5–1 at the Racecourse to reach an amazing 100 points for the season so far; Notts County won 3–0 against Wealdstone, reaching 97 points themselves. The National League hadn't seen anything like it.

Then, disaster. Out of the blue Wrexham lost to Halifax Town. Elliot had put the Red Dragons ahead in the first half, but poor finishing and some under par defending saw them ship three goals in the second half. Wrexham's unbelievable 28 game unbeaten run had come to an end. Worse still, Notts County had beaten Wealdstone 3–0 to move on to 100 points and take the top spot on goal difference.

Wrexham still had a game in hand, but County were in the driving seat. The next game was going to be very important for both teams: they would face each other at the Racecourse.

It was a game that could decide a season.

CHAPTER 21

GOING UP!

22 April 2023, Racecourse Ground

The game of the season had gone Wrexham's way.
Ben's heroics in goal and strikes from Paul, Elliot and
Jacob Mendy had clinched the vital win. They were
three points clear with a game in hand – promotion
was in Wrexham's hands. They drew 0–0 away at
Barnet, but it was a valuable point. Then a thumping
3–0 win against Yeovil meant that just one win
from their remaining two games would guarantee
promotion. Notts County were still picking up points,
but there was nothing they could do. It was in
Wrexham's hands, but could they hold on?

In North Wales, the excitement was building. The women's team had shown the men's how to do it, by winning promotion themselves; now the biggest crowd of the season packed the Racecourse Ground, hoping that the Red Dragons could clinch the top spot with a game to spare.

Of course, it wasn't only the inhabitants of Wrexham that were watching on. With celebrity owners and a popular documentary series on the television, Wrexham had more followers world-wide than most League clubs, never mind teams in the fifth tier.

Rob and Ryan were there of course. The money they had put into the club was paying dividends now. They had promised success and the team was about to deliver. Their friend, the actor Paul Rudd, famous for playing Ant-Man, was also at the Racecourse Ground, hoping to share in a great occasion. It all felt a long way from the doom and gloom of previous seasons.

There was mixed news on the starting line-up for Wrexham, though. As the team walked out into the raucous Racecourse pitch for the evening kick-off,

fans were relieved to see that Ben and Paul were
fit to play. The news was less positive for Ollie and
Jordan Tunnicliffe, who had both failed to shake off
their injuries. Their replacements had performed well
in previous games, though, and the atmosphere was
electric under the Wrexham floodlights.

Perhaps the atmosphere was too much. Sometimes
an occasion can be too big and can be a distraction for
the players the fans are trying to support. It seemed
this was the case in this game. Boreham Wood hadn't
turned up to be bit-part players in Wrexham's success
story. They were chasing a play-off place and needed a
point to guarantee success. They also had the tightest
defence in the division. And if the watching fans
needed any reminding of how useful Boreham Wood
were they didn't have long to wait.

GOOOOAAAAALLLLLLL!!!!!!!

The game had barely kicked off and the ball was
already nestling in the back of the net – the Wrexham
net! The Racecourse was stunned – this was not
sticking to the Hollywood script! A long ball from
midfield had bounced over the unfortunate Eoghan,

who then slipped allowing the Boreham Wood forward Lee Ndlovu to chip Ben and send the away fans into wild celebration.

"They're all over the place," Phil grumbled. "Play the game, not the occasion!"

It took a while for Phil's wise words to sink in. It took Wrexham nearly a quarter of an hour before they were playing with anything like their usual fluid style. By then the Red Dragons were starting to click. Ryan Barnett was finding some joy down the Wrexham right, beating the Boreham Wood defender and sending in a dangerous cross that found Elliot, completely unmarked in the six-yard box. Elliot wasn't going to miss an opportunity like that, and he buried his header past the opposition keeper.

GOOOOOAAAAALLLLLL!!!!!!!!!!!!

From the owner's seats to the stands the wave of relief was obvious. Wrexham were back on equal terms.

The goal did not mean Wrexham were dominating the game though. Chances were few and far between. Paul had an acrobatic overhead shot bounce wide. A minute later a deep ball into the Wrexham box caused panic and the resulting header flashed wide. The game was going from end to end; a couple of minutes after the Boreham Wood attack, Paul was forcing the Boreham keeper into a save down low by the post.

The first half ended with the game tied – good for Boreham Wood, not so good for Wrexham.

Wrexham looked lively in the second half. Ben's long throws were causing problems for the opposition, but the breakthrough came from another of the Red Dragons' stars, Paul.

Picking up the ball on the left wing, he quickly cut in, leaving the covering defender floundering in his wake. With the Boreham Wood player desperately trying to catch him, Paul drove into the box and let fly with an unstoppable, curving right foot shot that flew over the keeper's despairing dive and into the top right corner of the net!

GOOOOOAAAAAAAAAALLLLLLLLLLL!!!!!!!!!!!!

Paul charged towards the corner flag and slid on his knees in celebration. Soon he was mobbed by his teammates as the Racecourse went wild.

"You legend!" shouted Luke over the din.

"Well, that's 46 goals for the season, so yeah, I reckon I am," Paul replied with a cheeky wink and a laugh.

"*We've got Mullin... Super Paul Mullin...*" the crowd sang – including those Hollywood A-listers in the directors' box.

Two minutes later, Ollie's replacement, Sam Dalby, laid off a clever ball in the box to a charging Andy Cannon – who was brought down by the Boreham Wood defender.

PENALTY!!!!!!

The crowd leapt up as one, but no – the assistant referee's flag was up for offside! On the sidelines, Phil wheeled away from the pitch in frustration.

"That's got to be tight!" he fumed. There was still so much time to be played. Phil wanted another goal almost as much as he wanted the final whistle to blow – anything to secure the three points.

Then, to Phil's relief, it was Boreham's turn to be undone by a high ball. A bit of scrappy midfield action on the halfway line led to a scooped pass bouncing over the Boreham defender and into the path of Paul. His lightning pace took him away from the covering player and into the corner of the box, where he unleashed a thunderbolt of a strike with his favoured left foot. There was no stopping that! There was the magnificent sound of ball hitting net and that fraction of a second of silence before the crowd went mad with celebration.

GOOOOAAAAAALLLLLLLLLLLLLLLL!!!!!!!!!!

Super Paul Mullin had done it again. On the pitch the players leapt onto Paul, and in the directors' box, Rob, Ryan and Humphrey hugged each other. Surely this was the moment that Wrexham would bring their fifteen-year stay in the National League to an end. Phil looked to the heavens in grateful thanks and pumped his fists.

"So that'll be 47 goals then!" said Luke, smacking his star striker on the back in congratulations.

There would be no hat-trick for Paul though. With just over a minute of regular time to go, Phil pulled Paul from the field, allowing him to hear the appreciation from the crowd. It also gave Ollie a chance to come on as a sub and get in on the celebrations. He was disappointed that he hadn't been fit enough to start, but he was fit enough to finish.

The Racecourse was rocking with the Welsh fans singing.

"We are going, up, say we are going up!" rolled round and around the old ground, the crowd bouncing and clapping. Phil paced nervously on the touchline, virtually kicking every ball as the clock ticked through the five minutes of added on time.

The final whistle blew – Wrexham were champions!

The crowd surged onto the pitch to celebrate. Red and white flares were lit, the music blared over the PA system. Players and supporters danced in one big mass of bodies that covered a third of the field. They had realized the dream.

As there had been a good chance Wrexham might win the league, the trophy and winners' medals had been brought to North Wales in preparation. Once the crowd had been cleared from the pitch the presentation ceremony could begin. The team assembled on the pitch, champagne bottles to the ready, as Luke and Ben as captain and vice-captain took the handles of the trophy. The trophy was lifted high into the air. The crowd cheered and the champagne cascaded like rain over the elated players.

Job done!

CHAPTER 22

A NEW DAWN PART 2

Wrexham had been promoted in record-breaking style. They finished the season on 111 points, which was the highest ever recorded in the National League. They also won more games than any team had achieved before, getting the upper hand 34 times. That wasn't all. Paul's 9 goals in Wrexham's FA cup run that season saw him pick up the Golden Ball award for being the competition's leading goal scorer. There was a lot to celebrate that year, but for the long-suffering Wrexham fans the party was just beginning. After the initial joy of winning the league, there was the trophy parade to look forward to.

"Wow!" said Phil as he looked down from the top

deck of the open-top bus at the head of the parade. "Look at them all! There must be thousands of them!"

Lining the roads were people of all ages, waving flags, setting off red and white flares, singing and clapping. They had come from all over, travelling from across the UK as well as from abroad to celebrate with the club. People had been initially drawn in by the pulling power of their starry owners, but then became engrossed with the thrilling battle with Notts County for the title. And here they were – over 20,000 of them cheering on the three buses that crawled by.

On the first was the men's team, Paul at the front holding the cup aloft. Behind came the women's team – celebrating their own promotion of course – all the staff that had worked so hard behind the scenes to keep the club going, the families, and Rob and Ryan.

"This is what it means to them all," shouted Rob over the noise of the crowd.

"Yeah, we made the right choice," Ryan agreed. "Imagine what it will be like when we win the Premier League."

Although it was a joke, getting to the top division

was still the dream. And why not?

To reward the players Rob and Ryan took them on an all-expenses paid trip to Las Vegas! This was definitely not the kind of thing National League players were used to. Not everyone went; Phil and Steve turned the opportunity down. The boys didn't need their boss looming over their shoulder while they relaxed. Instead, Phil and Steve went off with the club staff to Portugal on holiday, as a thank you for what they had done that season. It was a great way to unwind after a thrilling, but exhausting year.

Of course, there's not a great deal of time to chill out after the end of one season and the start of the next. Phil was soon back in the office working to bring in new faces. Division 2 might be at the bottom of the league pyramid, but the squad was going to need an injection of quality if it was going to survive its first season back. There was preseason training, and friendly matches to organise, too.

The players, back from the fun of Las Vegas, were surprised to discover they were going to be back in

America for preseason. The documentary series being filmed about them had been a hit in the U.S.A. as well as the U.K., so it made sense to try and build a fan base in the States.

They were going to play two games on the East coast of America and two on the West. They would play a Chelsea 11 first, then a team from LA Galaxy. After that Wrexham were going to be included in a preseason cup competition with Manchester United in San Diego, and then finish with a game against an 11 from Rob's hometown club, Philadelphia Union. There would also be open training sessions so fans new and old could get close to their heroes.

The first game was a rude awakening after the parties of the previous month. Chelsea had a new manager in charge, Mauricio Pochettino, and his team were keen to impress their new boss. Although Wrexham tried hard, they were taken apart by their Premier League opposition, eventually losing 5–0. Still, it was the first game of preseason, so it didn't really matter.

The next game against LA Galaxy was the complete

opposite. Wrexham ran out comfortable 4–0 winners with goals from Elliot and Paul to go alongside strikes from Andy Cannon and Anthony Forde.

"Good to see you two have found your scoring boots," Phil joked to Paul and Elliot as they got changed.

Paul laughed. "Yeah, I'm starting to feel sharp again."

"Well, we're definitely going to need goals this season," Phil replied.

The next game was against Manchester United. The Premier League side was fielding mainly youth and reserve team players, but they did have the highly experienced Jonny Evans in the side. Despite this the match had set a stadium record for ticket sales and the crowd were excited. The game started well with Wrexham quickly taking control – but then disaster!

Paul jumped to head the ball on the edge of the box, but the United keeper clattered into him with a clumsy challenge. Paul landed on the ground in a heap and it was obvious something was badly wrong. On the sidelines Phil was going mad.

"What kind of challenge is that for a friendly!" he fumed. "And he only got a yellow! He should be off!"

Paul was helped off the pitch and taken to hospital to get checked out. In the meantime, Wrexham cruised to a 3–1 victory, with Ollie getting on the scoresheet for his first of preseason. They had won the tournament cup, but the news from the hospital took the edge off the celebrations – Paul had broken four ribs and punctured a lung! He would miss the start of the season – how would Wrexham cope without their leading goal scorer?

Wrexham's game against Philadelphia was a 1–1 draw, so that meant preseason had ended with two wins, a draw and a loss. Ordinarily Phil and the players would have been happy with that, but the injury to Paul was a definite blow. They would have to bring in reinforcements – at least in the short term – and the start of the new season was fast approaching.

Wrexham managed to bring in a couple of players before the season kicked off – the Huddersfield Town centre back Will Boyle, and Irish international

James McClean. James had played in the Premier League with Sunderland, so the fans hoped his experience would come in useful. However, there was no replacement for Paul by the time the first game came round.

The injury was not enough to distract from the excitement of the coming game. Wrexham were opening the season with a home game against MK Dons. The Red Dragons were back in the League and were ready to celebrate.

The opposition teams coming to North Wales wouldn't be the only change the fans would see this season. The Racecourse Ground had changed its name, for instance. The club had entered a sponsorship agreement with the STōK Cold Brew Coffee company and from July was called the STōK Racecourse. The storied old ground had upgraded its floodlights, too, ready for the new season.

The crowds were there in their numbers – Ryan was there too, this time with Hollywood pal and Wolverine actor Hugh Jackman. The pride and excitement were tangible as Luke led out his side

to their stirring anthem "Wrexham is the Name",
applauding the crowd.

The referee tossed the coin, and the teams took up
their positions. Phil stood motionless on the sidelines.
Luke took a deep breath and slowly exhaled. This was
what they'd worked so hard for. This was the dawn
of another new era. The referee put the whistle to his
lips and blew.

They were off!

Read on for a sneak preview of
another brilliant football story

GARETH BALE

Available now!

CHAPTER 1

THE NEW GALÁCTICO

'*El nuevo jugador de Real Madrid, Gareth Bale.*'
'Real Madrid's new player, Gareth Bale.' When
they called out his name, the stadium went wild.
Thousands of fans clapped and cheered their new
record signing. '*Bale! Bale! Bale!*' They chanted his
name, the name that many of them already had on
their shirts. Gareth couldn't believe it – this wasn't
even his debut. He wasn't out there flying down the
wing; he was wearing a suit. He could only guess
how amazing the atmosphere would be for a game.
As he got to his feet and walked up to the stage, he
took a long, deep breath and told himself to stay
calm. He was no longer the shy boy he once was,

but he wasn't yet used to this kind of attention.

But even the butterflies in his stomach couldn't stop the big smile on Gareth's face. This was it; the biggest club in the world and the home of the *Galácticos*, the biggest superstars in the world. Luis Figo, Ronaldo, Raúl, David Beckham, Cristiano Ronaldo… and now Gareth Bale. As a child, he'd sat with his father in the stands at his local ground Ninian Park watching his Uncle Chris play, pretending that it was the Bernabéu Stadium and that the Cardiff City team was the mighty Real Madrid. Now he was living out that fantasy and this time it was Gareth, not his uncle, who was the star.

As he approached the microphone, Gareth waved to the fans and then to his loved ones. It meant the world to him that they were all here for his big day: his mother Debbie and his father Frank, his granddad Dennis, his older sister Vicky, his best friend Ellis and, of course, his girlfriend Emma and their beautiful young daughter Alba. Without their endless support, he knew he would never have made it here.

When things settled down a bit, Gareth began: *'Es*

un sueño para mi jugar para Real Madrid. Gracias por esta gran acogida. ¡Hala Madrid!' These were the first Spanish words he'd learnt and, of course, the most important. He'd practised them for days so that even in the excitement, he wouldn't forget them: 'It's my dream to play for Real Madrid. Thank you for this big welcome. Come on, Madrid!' The noise was incredible, so loud that he'd had to pause halfway through.

And then came the moment everyone had been waiting for, especially Gareth. He'd imagined it so many times but this time it was real. The President of Real Madrid held up the famous white shirt and there was his name in big black letters across the back: 'BALE'. The cameras flashed and the crowd roared once more. He was a *Galáctico* now – the most expensive of them all – and so his old number 3 shirt was no longer good enough. As he had in his last season at Tottenham, now he wore number 11, the number of his childhood hero, the Manchester United wing wizard Ryan Giggs.

Michael Owen had worn number 11 at Real

Madrid in 2004, as had Arjen Robben in 2007. Gareth was proud to follow in their footsteps but he was determined to make that shirt his own. Watching the scenes around him, Gareth couldn't wait for the biggest challenge of his life. He was the most expensive player in the world and there would be a lot of pressure on him to join his teammate Cristiano Ronaldo as one of the very best players of all time.

As he did keepie-uppies on the Bernabéu pitch, Gareth thought back to his childhood days at Caedelyn Park. As a lightning-fast teenager in Wales, his family and coaches had predicted big things for him but no one had predicted this. At both Southampton and Tottenham, there had been difficult times when injuries looked like they might end Gareth's childhood dream. But the Welsh dragon had battled on and made it to the top.

CHAPTER 2

UNCLE CHRIS, CARDIFF CITY HERO

Gareth had hardly slept but he wasn't tired. He'd never been so excited. Today, on this autumn day in 1992, and for the first time in his life, he was off to watch his Uncle Chris – Chris Pike – play for Cardiff City. He'd seen him score a goal on the television once but never live at Ninian Park with thousands of other fans. Now that he was three, his dad, Frank, had decided that he was finally old enough to go to a game.

Gareth couldn't wait. The morning went so slowly as he watched the clock, and he begged it to fast-forward to 3 pm. To help the time pass, he made his sister stand in goal in the hallway and he took shots like his uncle. Vicky wasn't a very good keeper and the soft football kept whizzing past her. *GOAL! GOAL! GOAL! The crowd goes wild!* Finally at 1.45, Gareth stood ready at the front door, wearing the blue Cardiff City shirt and blue-and-white scarf that his uncle had given him for Christmas.

'Gareth, on the way to the ground you mustn't let go of your dad's hand,' his mum, Debbie, told him as she zipped up his coat and put gloves in the pockets. 'There'll be a lot of people there and you could easily get lost and miss the match. Now you don't want that, do you? So promise me, you won't let go of your dad's hand.'

'I promise, Mum!' But Gareth wasn't really listening to his worried mother. He was thinking about the football match and how many goals Uncle Chris would score. He was Cardiff's superstar striker, their top goalscorer for three years in a row, Gareth's dad had told him. If he was lucky, maybe Uncle Chris would score a hat-trick for him.

To get to Ninian Park, they had to take the train, which was an adventure in itself for a young child. They arrived at the local station in plenty of time to see the single carriage pull slowly up to the platform. Soon they were off, past the gate across the tracks that they used to get to Caedelyn Park. Then from the quiet, green spaces of Whitchurch they made their way towards the noisy, crowded city centre. Gareth stared out of the window as the view shifted from nice gardens to big, ugly buildings.

'Dad, how many times have you been to see Cardiff play? Five? Ten? A hundred?' he asked when he got bored of the view.

Frank laughed at the jump in numbers. 'I'm not sure, son, but it must be close to a hundred by now. I was going to watch the Bluebirds long before your uncle started playing for them... long before you were even born!'

At each stop on the route, the train got busier and busier, and louder and louder. By Cardiff Central station, fans were practising their chants and talking about the team's best tactics. There were many players that they didn't like but they all seemed to love Uncle Chris. From Ninian Park Station, it was a short walk to the ground but it took a long time because the streets were so busy.

The experience was even better than he'd hoped. Still holding his father's hand, Gareth went through the blue turnstiles, then up the blue steps to his blue seat. The pitch looked so big and the players looked so small as they warmed up below. He tried to find his uncle. There he was in the penalty area, taking shots at the goalkeeper. Gareth waved and waved but of course his uncle didn't see him. He was focused on the game, plus there were thousands of faces in the crowd.

As the game kicked off, the noise was incredible. The Cardiff City fans never stopped singing for their team. Gareth didn't know many of the words but he joined in with the clapping and the shouts of 'Come on, Cardiff!' He'd have to ask his father to teach him the songs later. After twenty minutes, a Cardiff defender played a long pass and suddenly Uncle Chris was through on goal. The fans started to rise from their seats, calling for him to score... but the goalkeeper ran out and made a good save to deny him. At half-time, the score was still 0–0 and his father was looking nervous next to him. But why? Gareth was sure that Uncle Chris would score a goal and win the match for them.

And he did. With time running out, the Cardiff winger dribbled down the right and crossed the ball high into the penalty area. Gareth followed the ball as it floated, as if in slow motion, through the air and on to the head of... Uncle Chris! He had jumped higher than the defender and the ball flew past the goalkeeper and into the top corner of the net. 1–0!

His uncle ran towards the Cardiff supporters to celebrate, waving his fists with joy. In the excitement, everyone was up on their feet and for a moment, Gareth couldn't see a thing. He tugged on his father's sleeve and Frank lifted his son on to his shoulders to get a better view. From up high,

Gareth cheered and cheered until his throat was sore. 'That's my uncle!' he told the fans around him. It was the greatest feeling in the world.

The game ended 1–0 and as they walked home, Gareth asked his father if they could go to the next game.

'Yes, if you behave yourself,' Frank replied with a grin, and took out the fixture list. 'Right, Cardiff are playing away at Bury next Saturday but the weekend after that, it'll be Gillingham at home.'

Two weeks?! He had to wait fourteen whole days?! It seemed like a lifetime. Oh well, if he couldn't watch football every day, he would play it every day, and if he played it every day, he'd get better and better until he became as good as his uncle. Or maybe even better.

When they got home, his mother opened the front door. 'Did you enjoy the game, son?' she asked, helping him out of his coat.

But it was a pointless question; she already knew the answer because Gareth was smiling so much. 'Mum, it was amazing! We won 1–0 and

Uncle Chris scored! When I grow up, I'm going to be a footballer just like him! Dad, can we go to the park tomorrow to practise?'

CHAPTER 3

GIGGSY IN THE GARDEN

'Giggsy's on the run, past one defender, then another...
and another! What an incredible run this is! He's
through on goal with just the keeper to beat. From
twenty yards out, he aims for the bottom corner...
What a goooooaaaaaaaallllll!'

Gareth turned away to celebrate, his Cardiff
City shirt lifted high up over his head, his arms
outstretched like an aeroplane. To complete his
routine, he did 'The Klinsmann', throwing him-self
down onto the grass, arms stretched out in front of
him like he was diving into a swimming pool. His
mum would be furious – more football kit covered
in mud and grass stains. His friend Ellis had hardly

moved in goal. It wasn't as much fun without real defenders but a goal was still a goal.

The aspiring footballer had been working hard on his shooting after school on his own, in the dark and often in the rain, hitting the ball as hard as he could at targets that he placed around the garden. It took time for him to find his accuracy, as a quick look next-door would show. Every day, Mr Tout would throw the footballs back over the fence but Gareth was too shy to knock on his door and ask for them. When he kicked one over, he'd hear his neighbour mutter and curse. The best Gareth could do was shout a quick 'Sorry!' and then run back into the house.

His parents weren't too happy either about the damage to their plants, but it was better than Gareth playing in the house. 'Gareth, go outside for a bit,' his father would say when he saw him fighting with his sister over what TV channel to watch. 'You've got too much energy.' Like a puppy, Gareth needed his exercise. Both of his parents were big sports fans and it was hard for them to complain about their son showing such an interest in something. But that didn't stop Debbie from wishing that Gareth cared as much about his times tables.

Gareth wasn't the worst student but he wasn't the best either. Like a lot of other seven-year-old boys, he was clever and did well when he tried hard, but there was usually something else on his mind. When he wasn't playing football, he was normally dreaming about it, or thinking about it. How would it feel to score the winning goal in a cup final? What would he need to do to become the best? He knew he was faster than the other kids he played against for Eglwys Newydd Primary School, but he had to work on his other skills like passing, dribbling, tackling and heading.

There was a long way to go if he was going to be as good as his new hero, Ryan Giggs. The Manchester United wizard was taking the Premier League by storm, making defenders look silly with his amazing abilities. Gareth loved watching him with the ball at his feet, moving one way and then the other – it was so exciting. 'That kid's got everything,' Gareth's father said one day when they watched Giggs on TV. 'In a year or two, he'll be one of the best in the world.' Gareth was sixteen years younger but they had three things in common: they were both Welsh, they were both left-footed wingers and they were both really fast. Anything was possible.

That was Gareth's dream, even at the age of six – to play against the best teams in the world and win lots of trophies. 'Practice makes perfect,' his other hero, Uncle Chris, would say as Gareth tried to dribble past him for the hundredth time. 'You were almost there that time – try it again. Remember, make your decision early and don't stop.' Come rain or shine, Gareth never gave up until he succeeded, even when he was out of breath, his face was red and sweaty, and his legs were heavy and painful. Even his mum calling him in for dinner couldn't stop Gareth. When it came to sport, he never ran out of energy.

Thank goodness, because Gareth was already in high demand. In Wales, rugby would always be the number one sport. At Caedelyn Park, for example, there were eight sets of rugby posts and only four football goals, although sometimes they'd use the space under the posts as a goal. The rugby coaches thought Gareth could be a great winger, even if he was a bit small and skinny for such a tough game. He was a good kicker and, of course, he had the speed to run the length of the pitch to score lots of tries.

Gareth wanted to play as many sports as possible, as often as possible, but his heart lay with football. He was just much more comfortable with a ball at his feet than he was with it in his hands. Frank, who had played both football and rugby as a boy, was very happy to let Gareth decide for himself. 'Son, I'll support you in whichever sport you choose to play. Unless it's ballet!'

For now, though, football in the garden was the main focus. 'Right, my turn!' his best friend Ellis shouted as he reached carefully into the rose bush to get the ball back. He hardly ever saved Gareth's shots; they were too powerful and accurate. Placing the ball down on the edge of the grass, Ellis began his commentary. 'Jamie Redknapp has the ball in midfield for Liverpool. He spots Robbie Fowler's run and plays a perfect pass. Fowler beats the centre- back with ease and he's through on goal! The keeper comes out... but he can't stop that. Gooooooooaaaaaaaalllllllllllll!'

As Ellis kissed the ground with delight, Gareth hit the ground with anger. Even messing about in his own back garden, he hated to lose. He should have saved it but only his fingertips could make contact with the ball. He'd had enough of this kick-about – he wanted to play a proper match
on a proper pitch with proper opponents. He wanted to have the space to run at defenders and score goals.

It was half-term and there was still a whole afternoon to play. It was perfect weather for football – not too hot, not too cold, no wind and no rain. Gareth picked up the ball and walked towards the gate. 'Shall we go and see if there's anyone down at the park? As long as we're back before it gets dark, my mum won't mind.'

MEET THE TEAM

1 ROB LAINTON

Position: GOALKEEPER
Nation: ENGLAND
D.O.B: 12 OCT 1989

3 CALLUM MACFADZEAN

Position: WING-BACK
Nation: SCOTLAND
D.O.B: 16 JAN 1994

4 BEN TOZER

Position: CENTRE-BACK
Nation: ENGLAND
D.O.B: 1 MAR 1990

5 AARON HAYDEN

Position: CENTRE-BACK
Nation: ENGLAND
D.O.B: 16 JAN 1997

6 JORDAN TUNNICLIFFE

Position: CENTRE-BACK
Nation: ENGLAND
D.O.B: 13 OCT 1993

7 JORDAN DAVIES

Position: WINGER
Nation: WALES
D.O.B: 18 AUG 1998

2023-24 SEASON

8 LUKE YOUNG

Position:	MIDFIELDER
Nation:	ENGLAND
D.O.B:	22 FEB 1993

9 OLLIE PALMER

Position:	STRIKER
Nation:	ENGLAND
D.O.B:	21 JAN 1992

10 PAUL MULLIN

Position:	STRIKER
Nation:	ENGLAND
D.O.B:	6 NOV 1994

11 LIAM MCALINDEN

Position:	MIDFIELDER
Nation:	IRELAND
D.O.B:	26 SEP 1993

12 GEORGE EVANS

Position:	MIDFIELDER
Nation:	ENGLAND
D.O.B:	13 DEC 1994

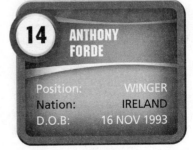

14 ANTHONY FORDE

Position:	WINGER
Nation:	IRELAND
D.O.B:	16 NOV 1993

15 EOGHAN O'CONNELL

Position:	CENTRE-BACK
Nation:	IRELAND
D.O.B:	13 AUG 1995

16 BILLY WALTERS

Position:	STRIKER
Nation:	ENGLAND
D.O.B:	15 OCT 1994

17 BRYCE HOSANNAH

Position:	WING-BACK
Nation:	ENGLAND
D.O.B:	8 APR 1999

18 SAM DALBY

Position:	STRIKER
Nation:	ENGLAND
D.O.B:	7 DEC 1999

19 JACOB MENDY

Position:	WING-BACK
Nation:	GAMBIA
D.O.B:	27 DEC 1996

20 ANDY CANNON

Position:	MIDFIELDER
Nation:	ENGLAND
D.O.B:	14 MAR 1996

21 MARK HOWARD

Position: GOALKEEPER
Nation: ENGLAND
D.O.B: 21 SEP 1986

22 THOMAS O'CONNOR

Position: MIDFIELDER
Nation: IRELAND
D.O.B: 21 APR 1999

23 JAMES MCCLEAN

Position: WINGER
Nation: IRELAND
D.O.B: 22 APR 1989

25 WILL BOYLE

Position: CENTRE-BACK
Nation: ENGLAND
D.O.B: 1 SEP 1995

26 STEVEN FLETCHER

Position: STRIKER
Nation: SCOTLAND
D.O.B: 26 MAR 1987

27 JAKE BICKERSTAFF

Position: STRIKER
Nation: ENGLAND
D.O.B: 11 SEP 2001

29 RYAN BARNETT

Position:	WINGER
Nation:	ENGLAND
D.O.B:	23 SEP 1999

30 JAMES JONES

Position:	MIDFIELDER
Nation:	SCOTLAND
D.O.B:	13 FEB 1996

31 LUKE MCNICHOLAS

Position:	GOALKEEPER
Nation:	IRELAND
D.O.B:	1 JAN 2000

32 MAX CLEWORTH

Position:	CENTRE-BACK
Nation:	ENGLAND
D.O.B:	9 AUG 2002

33 ARTHUR OKONKWO

Position:	GOALKEEPER
Nation:	ENGLAND
D.O.B:	9 SEP 2001

34 AARON JAMES

Position:	CENTRE-BACK
Nation:	ENGLAND
D.O.B:	30 JUN 2005

35 OWEN CUSHION

Position: MIDFIELDER
Nation: ENGLAND
D.O.B: 5 JAN 2005

38 ELLIOT LEE

Position: MIDFIELDER
Nation: ENGLAND
D.O.B: 16 DEC 1994

39 DANIEL DAVIES

Position: LEFT-BACK
Nation: WALES
D.O.B: 20 NOV 2004

41 LIAM HALL

Position: GOALKEEPER
Nation: ENGLAND
D.O.B: 18 DEC 2004

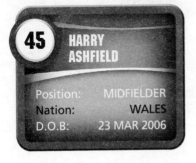

45 HARRY ASHFIELD

Position: MIDFIELDER
Nation: WALES
D.O.B: 23 MAR 2006

52 CALLUM EDWARDS

Position: STRIKER
Nation: ENGLAND
D.O.B: 22 JUN 2006

WREXHAM AFC HONOURS

League

🏆 Third Division: 1977–78

🏆 National League: 2022–23

🏆 The Combination: 1900–01, 1901–02, 1902–03, 1904–04

🏆 Welsh Senior League: 1894–95, 1895–96

Cup

🏆 Football League Trophy: 2004–05

🏆 FA Trophy: 2012–13

🏆 Football League North Cup: 1943–44

🏆 FAW Premier Cup: 1997–98, 1999–2000, 2000–01, 2002–03, 2003–04

🏆 Welsh Cup: 1877–78, 1882–83, 1892–93, 1896–97, 1902–03, 1904–05, 1908–09, 1909–10, 1910–11, 1913–14, 1914–15, 1920–21, 1923–24, 1924–25, 1930–31, 1956–57, 1957–58, 1959–60, 1971–72, 1974–75, 1977–78, 1985–86, 1994–95

GREATEST MOMENTS

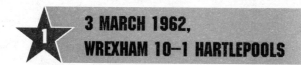

1

3 MARCH 1962,
WREXHAM 10–1 HARTLEPOOLS

Three different players – Wyn Davies, Roy Ambler and
Ron Barnes – scored hat-tricks as the Red Dragons
crushed Hartlepools by an incredible 10 goals to one.
Davies, whose three goals came inside the first 24
minutes, would go on to play for both Manchester
City and Manchester United, as well as winning 34
caps for Wales.

22 SEPTEMBER 1976,
TOTTENHAM HOTSPUR 2–3 WREXHAM

Wrexham were in the Third Division – then the third tier of the Football League – when they were drawn against top-tier giants Tottenham Hotspur in the League Cup, a team which included Pat Jennings and Glenn Hoddle. Wrexham raced into a 3–0 lead with two goals from Mickey Thomas and one from Billy Ashcroft, and although the Londoners clawed two goals back, it was the Welsh team who won the day.

6 FEBRUARY 1978,
WREXHAM 4–1 NEWCASTLE UTD

Wrexham were well on their way to winning the Third Division trophy when they met Newcastle United in the fourth round of the FA Cup; Newcastle on the other hand were facing relegation, and the teams would meet next season in the Second Division. Goals from Dixie McNeil, Bobby Shinton and Les Cartwright delivered a famous victory for the Welsh giant-killers.

22 APRIL 1978,
WREXHAM 7–1 ROTHERHAM UTD

Wrexham celebrated their already-assured promotion to the Second Division with a stunning late-season demolition of struggling Rotherham United. Five goals without reply by the 34th minute knocked the stuffing out of the visitors; Les Cartwright made four of the seven goals and scored one himself as the party started at the Racecourse Ground.

3 OCTOBER 1984,
FC PORTO 4–3 WREXHAM

Wrexham had slipped into the Fourth Division when they were drawn against FC Porto in the European Cup Winners' Cup. The Portuguese giants were 3–0 up at home when Jake King scored either side of the interval; Paolo Futre made it 4–2; and club legend Barry Horne netted in the 88th minute to make it 4–3 – sending Wrexham through on away goals thanks to a 1–0 home win.

6 4 JANUARY 1992,
WREXHAM 2–1 ARSENAL

An Arsenal team containing players like David
Seaman, David O'Leary, Tony Adams and Paul Merson
arrived at the Racecourse Ground expecting an easy
FA Cup win against a struggling Wrexham side. Alan
Smith gave the visitors the lead before the break, but
a stunning free-kick from veteran Mickey Thomas and
a poached goal by Steve Watkin completed an epic
comeback for the Red Dragons.

7 10 APRIL 2005,
SOUTHEND 0–2 WREXHAM

Wrexham's financial troubles – the club was £2.6m
in debt – had resulted in a 10-point deduction that
would eventually see the club relegated to League Two.
But, inspired by an excellent display from 22-year-old
goalkeeper Ben Foster, on loan to the Red Dragons from
Stoke City, Wrexham defeated Southend to win the
Football League Trophy for the first time.

26 MARCH 2022, WREXHAM 6–5 DOVER ATHLETIC

Dover Athletic arrived at the Racecourse Ground bottom of the table, and goals from Paul Mullin and James Jones saw Wrexham two goals up within 20 minutes. But at half-time, Dover were 5–2 in front! Ollie Palmer gave the home team hope with two goals, before Jordan Davies scored a brace of his own in extra time to complete an incredible comeback.

7 JANUARY 2023, COVENTRY CITY 3–4 WREXHAM

The latest entry in Wrexham's proud history of giant-killing came with a stunning away win at Championship side Coventry City in the FA Cup. Sam Dalby and Elliot Lee put the visitors ahead, and Tom O'Connor's goal meant they were 3–1 up at half time. Despite a spirited Coventry fightback, Paul Mullin's penalty kick saw the Red Dragons run out 4–3 winners.

10 APRIL 2023, WREXHAM 3–2 NOTTS COUNTY

A clash of the titans at the Racecourse Ground was effectively the title decider: two teams tied on 100 points, having both scored exactly 106 goals. In an epic game, Notts County took the lead, Wrexham equalised, then went ahead – only for the Magpies to draw level once more. Elliot Lee's winner, and Ben Foster's penalty save, proved decisive.

22 APRIL 2023, WREXHAM 3–1 BOREHAM WOOD

Wrexham clinched promotion to the Football League after 15 years in non-league football with victory over Boreham Wood at the Racecourse Ground. A goal in the first minute for the visitors tested the Red Dragons' nerves, but an equalizer from Elliot Lee and a second-half brace for star striker Paul Mullin sent the Welsh fans into dreamland.

TEST YOUR KNOWLEDGE

QUESTIONS

1. Who was the manager of Wrexham AFC when Ryan and Rob took over the club?

2. How much did Paul Mullin cost from Cambridge United?

3. Which trophy has Wrexham won a record 23 times?

4. What is the name of the stand at the Racecourse Ground that the new owners decided to rebuild?

5. What skill is the trademark of Ben Tozer?

6. Who became Wrexham's record signing when he joined from AFC Wimbledon in January 2022?

7. Which team defeated Wrexham in the play-off semi-final to deny them promotion in 2022?

8. Which player scored two goals on his debut for Wrexham against Eastleigh in 2022?

9. How many goals were scored in total in Wrexham's home victory over Barnet in October 2022?

10. How many points did Wrexham finish with in their promotion season?

11. What is the nickname of Wrexham's rivals Notts County?

Answers below . . . No cheating!

1. *Dean Keates* **2.** *Nothing – it was a free transfer* **3.** *The Welsh Cup* **4.** *The Kop* **5.** *Long throws* **6.** *Ollie Palmer* **7.** *Grimsby Town* **8.** *Elliot Lee* **9.** *Twelve* **10.** *One hundred and eleven* **11.** *The Magpies*

CAN'T GET ENOUGH OF
ULTIMATE FOOTBALL HEROES?

Check out heroesfootball.com
for quizzes, games, and competitions!

Plus join the Ultimate Football Heroes
Fan Club to score exclusive content and
be the first to hear about
new books and events.
heroesfootball.com/subscribe/